THE SILVER CANARY

THE SIGNAL. THE SHIFT. THE NEW SYSTEM

MICHAEL MACDONALD

First Edition

For my boys, I love you both more than words can hold. May these pages inspire you, steady you, and prepare you to build a bright future with courage, clarity, and wisdom.

CONTENTS

THE 3D READ

A GODTONE SOUNDTRACK

3D READ pairs the book with a purpose-built soundtrack so you stay calm, focused, and in flow while you read.

GodTone is the continuous background layer that supports regulation, clarity, and mental stamina from start to finish.

1) FLOW (INSTRUMENTAL)
Music for deep focus while you read.

2) IGNITION (LYRICAL)
A chapter-end song that locks in the message.

Flow

Ignition

PROLOGUE
GHOST WEEK

The first sign rarely arrives with alarms. It arrives as friction.

A routine buy turns into a conversation, the kind that feels normal until it does not. The quote on the screen looks clean. The numbers behave. The world keeps moving.

Then you ask the only question that matters.

"How fast can it ship?"

There is a pause. A small one. A professional one. The kind a person uses when they are choosing which version of the truth will cause the least disturbance.

"Lead times are shifting."

A harmless phrase. Smooth edges. Clean suit. It lands like a feather and carries the weight of a brick.

You press a little. Size. Delivery. Availability.

The price on the screen stays calm. The premium does not.

A spread opens in a place most people never look. A gap forms between what is quoted and what is real. You can still place an order. The language stays polite. The system stays confident. But the physical market starts speaking in its own dialect.

Limited. Allocation. Delay. Substitute. Check back tomorrow. Different product. Different terms.

The product is the same metal. The feeling is different.

That is the moment the room changes temperature.

It is subtle. Almost boring. That is why it works.

Most people stay focused on the theater. The chart, the candles, the commentators, the confident voiceovers insisting everything is functioning as expected. They read the headline and call it a day.

But the real signal comes from the places that touch the ground.

A dealer hesitates. A premium stretches. Inventory thins. Delivery timelines drift. The screen stays smooth while the supply chain tightens like a fist closing slowly.

You learn something important in that moment.

Markets can be managed. Messaging can be managed. Screens can be managed.

Physical behavior reveals what confidence is covering.

That is when you stop asking, "What is the price?"

And you start asking, "What is availability telling me?"

Because when the metal becomes difficult, it is rarely about the metal.

It is about trust.

It is about settlement.

It is about the difference between a claim and a thing.

And once you see that difference clearly, you begin to recognize a pattern.

Certain weeks carry a strange stillness. The narrative stays calm, the charts behave, and yet the underlying mechanisms start adjusting in quiet ways.

Some weeks do not feel dangerous while you are living them.

They feel normal.

The news scrolls. Markets move. People go to work. Bills get paid. The system hums along the way it always has. Same sky. Same roads. Same conversations.

And yet, beneath that normal surface, pressure builds.

Not the kind of pressure you can photograph. The kind you can sense if you know what to watch for. The kind that shows up in spreads and premiums, in quiet shortages, in policy whispers, in the way officials start choosing their words more carefully.

Ghost Week is what I call those stretches of time when the system is stressed but still smiling. When the narrative stays calm, but reality tightens. When the public is distracted, but the smartest money is already repositioning. When you can feel the room temperature change even though nobody opened a door.

During Ghost Week, the surface story stays smooth. It has to. Confidence is not just a feeling. Confidence is infrastructure. It is the thin set of beams holding up the space between stability and chaos. So the public gets a story designed to keep them steady.

But the physical world does not care about stories.

Silver does not move like a pure commodity in moments like these. It moves like a signal. A canary. A truth device. It reveals stress in the system before the system admits the stress exists.

That is why the silver market gets weird first. Not always in the price on a screen. Screens can be managed. Screens can be delayed.

The real signal is what happens when you try to buy. When you try to take delivery. When the premium changes faster than the quote. When inventory thins. When supply starts feeling rationed by invisible hands.

This is when the gap between paper and physical gets louder. This is when the system whispers before it screams.

Most people miss it because they are trained to watch the wrong signal. They watch the price. They watch the headlines. They watch the narrative.

But the canary sings in the physical market first.

And when it sings, you should pay attention. Not with panic. With awareness.

Ghost Week is not about predicting collapse. It is about reading the air. Recognizing trust thinning. Noticing the rails beneath money shifting. Realizing the old assumptions are becoming more expensive to maintain.

If you learn to recognize Ghost Week, you stop being surprised by the next era. You start seeing it coming.

And that is what this book is.

A map.

A way to see what is real.

A way to understand the signal, the shift, and the new system while most people are still arguing about the old one.

SIGNALCHECK

A Reader Orientation

There was a time when silver whispered.

It showed up in small frictions. In premiums that drifted higher than they should. In delivery windows that stretched just long enough to make you pause. In the quiet sense that the screen price and the real price were beginning to walk in different directions.

That time has passed.

The signal no longer requires belief. It shows up in behavior. In repetition. In what people are doing quietly and at scale, even while the official story stays calm.

And calm is where markets mislead the best.

This book is built around one simple idea: silver behaves like a canary in the monetary system. Not because it predicts the future perfectly, but because it reacts honestly to stress.

Silver cannot be coached into compliance.

It cannot pretend away constraint.

It must be mined, refined, shipped, stored, delivered.

It must exist somewhere, under someone's control, at a specific moment in time.

Claims can trade endlessly.

Settlement cannot.

This section anchors the book to the world you are standing in now, without turning the rest of the manuscript into a moving target. You do not need a new worldview. You do not need hype.

You need a clean way to read what is already happening.

Here are the five realities that matter most in this moment. They are also the spine of what follows.

1 Structural deficit

A shortage is loud. A structural deficit is patient.

A structural deficit does not mean silver disappears. It means the flow is insufficient to satisfy competing demands without drawing down buffers that were never meant to be exhausted.

The system can still function, but it begins functioning differently.

It rations through time and terms before it rations through price. Lead times stretch. Minimums rise. Substitution becomes normal. Friction becomes familiar.

This is not a morality tale. It is physics.

When replacement is slower than use, time becomes a cost. The question shifts from What is the price? to Can I get it when I need it, under terms I can live with?

That shift changes behavior long before it changes sentiment.

2 Paper-physical divergence

Paper silver and physical silver exist in the same ecosystem, but they do not serve the same purpose.

Paper is designed for exposure. It offers access, liquidity, convenience. It smooths volatility. It makes the market look deep and continuous.

Physical is designed for settlement.

It occupies space. It incurs cost. It is consumed in industry. It cannot be scaled elastically. It cannot be netted away.

These realities can coexist as long as most participants remain content with representation instead of resolution. Divergence begins when that preference shifts.

A spike in premiums during chaos is normal.

Persistent premiums during calm are information.

Price reflects consensus.

Divergence reflects strain.

3 Inventory migration

Before anything becomes scarce, it relocates.

Silver does not vanish. It migrates.

It moves from open pools to closed hands. From shared custody to direct custody. From locations optimized for liquidity to locations optimized for certainty.

That is not panic. It is optimization under changing assumptions.

When trust is evenly distributed, inventory circulates freely. When trust becomes uneven, chains shorten. Custody preferences harden. Jurisdictions differentiate.

A bar that exists but will not circulate is functionally different from a bar that exists to settle claims.

Accounting may treat them as equal.

The delivery system does not.

4 Trust erosion

Trust rarely collapses. It thins.

It thins through terms. Through clauses. Through steps that did not exist last year and now arrive with explanations polished enough to sound rehearsed.

Systems under stress do not announce weakness. They redesign responsibility.

They add layers.

They add approvals.

They add exceptions that become policy.

Most people notice only when it touches them personally. A transfer that takes longer. A withdrawal that requires review. A limit that appears without warning.

This is the operational shape of trust erosion.

Silver matters here because it forces a question modern systems try to retire:

What do you actually own, and can you prove it when it matters?

5 Programmable money risk

Programmable systems are efficient until trust becomes uneven.

Money that can be filtered, delayed, conditioned, or restricted is often framed as a technological upgrade. In stable environments, it feels like progress.

The stress shows up when rules change faster than expectations.

Then the question becomes blunt:

Who decides what you can do with your money?

This is not an argument against technology. It is an argument for finality. For assets and structures that do not require permission to exist or settle.

Silver does not compete on speed.

It competes on final settlement.

How to use this book right now

Read for pattern, not persuasion.

If you read this like a debate, your brain will try to win. Read it like weather. You do not argue with wind. You notice it. You respect it. You adjust.

Read for mechanics.

Underline lead times, custody rules, settlement language, inventory behavior, and terms. Those are the places where systems confess the truth.

Do not chase the perfect moment.

The perfect entry is a myth that steals years. Structurally tightening systems punish procrastination more than imperfect timing.

Keep your nervous system on your side.

Receipts are meant to ground you, not agitate you. A steady mind reads reality better than a flooded one.

You are not looking for one dramatic confirmation.

You are looking for clustering.

Repetition.

Signals pointing in the same direction over time.

The canary does not reward speed.

It rewards preparation.

This is not a call to action.

It is a call to awareness.

With that orientation in place, the rest of the book can do what it was designed to do.

Now we go into the chapters.

INTRODUCTION
THE SIGNAL, THE SHIFT, AND THE NEW SYSTEM

I Bring Receipts

Before we begin, I want to give you one thing upfront: proof.

In 2012, I published a book called *The Silver Bomb*. In it, I outlined a pattern I believed would eventually surface in the silver market. Not as a theory, but as a consequence of how debt-based systems behave under pressure.

One of the central ideas was simple, and at the time it sounded extreme to most people: the quoted "price" of silver could drift away from the real-world cost of obtaining physical metal. Paper silver and physical silver were not the same thing, and the gap between them could widen as stress increased.

That book is still public. Anyone can verify it. The record has been sitting in plain sight for more than a decade.

Today, that phenomenon is no longer theoretical. You can see it in premiums, in availability, in delivery delays, and in the growing distance between what the screen suggests and what the real market demands.

I'm sharing that context for a reason. In a world flooded with opinions, what matters is pattern recognition, structure, and receipts.

This book is the next phase of that original warning, written for the world we are standing in now.

Now let me tell you where this really began for me.

I did not start in finance. I started in the real world, in work that had weight and consequence. Construction teaches you something quickly: reality does not negotiate. Measurements either match or they do not. Foundations either hold or they fail.

That mindset became the first lens that ever made money feel strange.

I left construction and moved into sales because I wanted a stronger future for my family. That shift taught me something most people only learn after they have been burned: trust is the real product. People move on emotion first, then justify with logic.

Then I overheard a conversation about precious metals that opened a door. I went in thinking it was a sales opportunity. I came out realizing it was a civilization question.

Money is not what people think it is. Money is not a paper bill. Money is not a digital balance. Money is trust, made visible. And trust can be engineered.

Once you see that, you start asking a question that changes the way you watch the world:

What happens when the conditions change?

That question took me deep into monetary history, central banking, and the lifecycle of currencies. It took me into precious metals. It eventually led me to Bitcoin too, because Bitcoin represents a modern attempt to solve the same old trust problem using a new rail.

And that brings us to the story you and I are living now.

We are entering the next monetary era. Debt is too large to resolve cleanly. Supply chains are becoming strategic. New settlement systems are being built. Money is becoming more programmable.

In early eras, trust feels thick. The rules feel consistent. Saving feels meaningful. Planning feels rational.

In late eras, trust thins. Interventions become normal. The system must work harder to maintain the appearance of stability.

That is why the title matters.

Silver is the signal. It does not behave like a normal commodity when trust is thinning. It reveals stress early, often through the physical market, even when screens look calm.

The shift is what happens next. When trust thins, the system chooses speed over discipline. It leans into control, incentives, and managed behavior because those tools work fast.

The new system arrives as a hybrid. Old rails still run, while new rails steadily capture territory. Settlement becomes more strategic. Access becomes more conditional. The definition of money becomes less uniform.

So this book is a map.

It is designed to help you recognize the signal, understand the shift, and position yourself intelligently for the new system, with structure rather than fear.

Because the people who thrive in transition eras are the people who see clearly. They reduce fragility. They build options. They own proof.

If you are reading this, you are already ahead.

Let's go the rest of the way.

THE SILVER CANARY FRAMEWORK

How to Read This Book

This book is built on a simple idea.

Most people watch the world through headlines.

Smart people watch it through patterns.

The people who thrive watch it through structure.

The Silver Canary framework is a way to see what is happening beneath the noise, so you can position yourself with clarity instead of reaction.

It has three layers.

1) THE SIGNAL

Silver is not only a metal. It is a diagnostic tool.

When trust begins thinning, silver tends to reveal stress early, often through real-world friction instead of the screen price.

Reader instruction:

Watch what happens at the point of reality, when people move from exposure to delivery.

That is where the signal appears first.

2) THE SHIFT

When the signal appears, behavior changes.

Trust starts repricing.

Institutions protect themselves quietly.

Governments choose words more carefully.

The public feels pressure without always knowing why.

This is the phase where interventions become normal, incentives replace discipline, and control expands because control is faster than rebuilding trust.

The shift is not a moment.

It is a turning.

Reader instruction:

Track behavior, not commentary. Behavior is where the truth leaks first.

3) THE NEW SYSTEM

When behavior turns, new rails get built.

Money is not only currency.

Money is also settlement.

Money is also access.

Money is also custody.

Money is also control.

The new system arrives as a hybrid. Old rails remain, but new rails steadily take territory. Digital settlement expands. Programmable money becomes more common. Transparency increases in some areas, while conditional access expands in others.

In this world, the most valuable asset is not prediction.

It is options. Options that do not depend on the story staying believable.

Reader instruction:

Build optionality in your life and finances, because optionality is freedom in transition eras.

If you can read these three layers, you stop being surprised.

You start seeing what is coming.
You stop reacting.
You start positioning.
That is the purpose of this book.
Real work has weight.
Real money should too.

CHAPTER 1

WHEN MONEY LOST ITS WEIGHT

The first time I realized money was strange, I was holding a hammer.

Not a symbolic hammer. A real one. Heavy in the hand. Honest. It did not care who I was. It did not care what I believed. It did its job.

That is what construction teaches you.

There is no spokesperson to spin the result. No policy that edits the laws of physics. Reality does not negotiate.

It teaches you something quieter too.

You can work hard, stay disciplined, do everything right, and still feel like the finish line keeps moving.

That feeling was my first crack in the story of money.

I was not thinking about macroeconomics. I was thinking about my life, my family, my future. I had spent years building things people could touch, but I wanted a career that could build something bigger for the people I loved. I wanted to move from survival to strength.

So I got into sales.

Car sales first.

I did well. Not because I was a shark, but because I was steady. Because I listened. Because people could feel I was trying to help them make a decision they could live with, not win a trick.

Even then, I knew it was a stepping stone.

Then I overheard a conversation that opened a door.

A manager was talking about his brother-in-law selling precious metals. Gold and silver. I barely knew what that meant. In my head, precious metals belonged to history. Old coins. Museums. Something that lived in the past.

But the manager was talking about money.

Real money.

Not commissions. Not a good month. The kind of money that changes how a man breathes.

My brain leaned in the way it always does when it senses a doorway.

I started investigating.

At first, it was simple. It was sales. I understood sales. If people were making money selling gold and silver, I wanted to know why.

But the deeper I went, the clearer it became.

The real product was not metal.

The real product was a truth most people do not study until they are forced to.

Money is not what people think it is.

Money is not a piece of paper. Money is not a number on a screen.

Money is trust.

And trust can be engineered.

I fell into the rabbit hole the way a man falls into gravity. Suddenly the invisible becomes obvious. Suddenly you can feel the rules holding everything up.

I learned about fiat currency. About the shift away from hard money. About the lifecycle of currencies, and how they tend to break for the same reasons: debt, war, and the temptation to print stability.

I learned how credit expansion can feel like prosperity in the short term while it quietly builds fragility underneath.

I read everything I could get my hands on. The books people avoid because they do not make you feel smarter. They make you feel awake.

Then I did something that made the whole theory physical.

I held my first one-ounce gold coin.

Later, my first one-ounce silver coin.

If you have never held real metal, it is hard to explain the clarity it brings. It is not mystical. It is not poetry. It is simple.

Weight. Density. Presence.

Gold feels like permanence in your hand. It does not rust. It does not decay. It does not beg for confidence. It just sits there, quietly indifferent, like a law of nature.

Silver feels different. More grounded. More human. The people's metal. Real money in a form you can actually use. A metal with history and utility, living in two worlds at once: monetary and industrial.

Holding those coins did something to me.

It made everything else I had been calling money feel lighter than it should have been.

Not physically.

Psychologically.

It depended on belief. It depended on rules. It depended on the system continuing to function the way it always had.

That is when money started feeling conditional.

Like a stage set that looks solid until you walk behind it.

That realization did not make me paranoid.

It made me curious.

Because when you discover something is conditional, you start asking the only question that matters.

What happens when the conditions change?

That question changed my career. It changed what I read. It changed how I watched the world.

I went into precious metals sales and did well. I learned everything I could. I opened my own brokerage. I became the guy who would not shut up about gold and silver, because once something becomes real to you, you want other people to see it too.

And then the rabbit hole did what it always does.

It led to another door.

Bitcoin.

At first, I was skeptical. I still am, in the healthy way. But I also understood what Bitcoin represented: a modern response to an ancient problem. A digital attempt to solve the trust issue. A new rail.

And once you see the world through rails, the story gets bigger.

Silver is the signal. The rails are shifting. And the future is being built underneath our feet.

This chapter exists for one reason.

So you understand this is lived for me.

It started with a hammer. It moved through sales. It moved into metals. It moved into the deepest question a civilization can ask:

What is money?

And once you ask it, you do not get to un-ask it.

Because from that point on, you start watching the world like a builder.

Not like a spectator.

You start respecting structure. You start noticing stress. You start owning proof. You start positioning yourself for the world that is coming, not the world that used to be.

Silver does not predict collapse.

Silver reveals the moment trust turns thin. It reveals the moment access becomes conditional. It reveals the moment a promise starts behaving like a maybe.

Most people miss that moment because the screens stay calm and the voices stay confident.

But the physical market cannot fake its body language.

And once you learn to read that body language, you stop needing permission to see what is happening.

That is where this story begins.

CHAPTER 2
THE CANARY

Markets are forward-looking. They are not just reacting. They are constantly trying to sniff out what is coming next.

A market is like a fortune teller with a nervous system.

Markets do not predict the future like a mystic. They do something more useful.

They react before the public does.

They price what they sense. What they fear. What they anticipate. What they can no longer ignore.

They move ahead of headlines. Ahead of speeches. Ahead of the tidy explanations built afterward to make the move feel reasonable.

When you learn to read that early movement, you stop seeing the market as a scoreboard. You start seeing it as a nervous system.

It tightens first.

It twitches first.

It tells the truth early, long before anyone is willing to say the truth out loud.

Silver is one of the clearest examples of that.

Not because it is the biggest market.

Not because it is glamorous.

Silver rarely gets center stage. Stocks get obsession. Real estate gets worship. Gold gets reverence.

Silver gets treated like a side character.

And that is exactly why it matters.

Silver has a habit.

It moves first.

Not because it is emotional.

Because it is honest.

Silver spikes.

Silver snaps.

Silver throws flares.

Silver sits at an intersection most assets never touch. It is a monetary metal and an industrial necessity. It lives in vaults and it lives inside machines. It is a store of value and a physical input.

That combination makes it sensitive to stress in a way gold cannot replicate.

Gold can rise on monetary fear alone. It can climb slowly and dignified for years while the public barely notices.

Silver does not do dignified.

Silver moves like pressure.

Because silver is tied to parts of the real world that do not care what anyone believes.

Manufacturing.

Supply chains.

Energy.

Electronics.

Defense.

Medicine.

Infrastructure.

When silver tightens, it is not just reflecting investor mood. It is reflecting physical reality.

And physical reality is the one thing paper systems struggle to manage.

This is where most people misunderstand modern finance.

They think it is money moving around the system.

It is not.

Modern finance is claims moving around the system.

Claims on bonds.

Claims on mortgages.

Claims on cash flow.

Claims on commodities.

Claims on the claims.

Abstraction is efficient. It allows scale. It allows liquidity. It lets a modern economy function without hauling pallets of goods through every transaction.

The symbols are useful.

Until the symbols get mistaken for the thing itself.

In calm periods, that confusion does not cost much. The system works because most people accept the substitute. They accept the claim as if it were the underlying reality.

Under stress, that changes.

People stop caring about exposure.

They start caring about delivery.

They stop asking, "What is the price?"

They start asking, "Can I actually get it?"

That is where silver becomes dangerous.

Because silver is one of the few markets where a meaningful number of participants care about the physical object, not just the chart. Silver is a trade and a necessity.

And necessities have their own gravity.

They do not negotiate with narratives. They pull on the system until the system either provides supply or breaks trust.

This is why silver is the canary.

A canary does not cause the gas leak.

It reveals it.

Silver does not create financial stress.

It reveals it.

It reveals the gap between paper claims and physical availability.

It reveals the cost of pretending supply is infinite.

It reveals the cost of multiplying promises beyond reality.

And when that gap becomes visible, silver does something else.

It forces response.

I want you to understand that clearly because everything that follows depends on it.

The system does not fear gold the way it fears silver.

Gold is largely stored. It can sit in vaults and function as a reserve without disrupting production. It can be accumulated quietly.

Silver is different.

Silver is small enough to be squeezed and essential enough to matter. When demand surges, it collides with industrial supply chains immediately.

Silver is consumed.

Gold is largely stored.

When something is consumed, it must be replaced. When something is essential, it becomes non-negotiable.

That is the canary effect.

The signal spreads awareness of stress.

And once stress is perceived, behavior shifts.

That is where we go next.

CHAPTER 3

THE PAPER METAL MACHINE

If you have never watched the precious metals market from the inside, it is easy to assume it works the way people imagine markets work.

Buyers.

Sellers.

A price floating somewhere in the middle.

That picture is comforting because it feels fair.

It is also wrong.

Silver is priced by paper.

The price you see is a number produced by contracts, leverage, and promises, not by people trading bars hand to hand.

Once you understand that, the subject changes.

Because then you have to ask the question most people never ask.

What exactly is being traded?

The answer is not metal.

The answer is promises.

Contracts.

Derivatives.

Synthetic exposure.

Financial instruments designed to behave like silver without requiring anyone to move a single bar from one place to another.

In a physical market, scarcity shows up quickly. Less supply pushes price higher until supply returns or demand breaks.

In a paper market, scarcity can be delayed.

Disguised.

Absorbed.

Paper makes scarcity negotiable. Paper makes time stretch.

This is not conspiracy.

It is structure.

Abstraction creates speed. Liquidity. Leverage.

People want exposure without storage. Profit without logistics. Hedges without friction.

That abstraction is useful.

It also creates a problem that only appears when the system is stressed.

Paper can multiply. Metal cannot.

You can create new paper claims on silver in seconds. Expand exposure. Expand apparent supply. Expand promises.

Physical silver does not work like that.

Mining takes years.

Refining has constraints.

Recycling has limits.

Inventories have boundaries.

Supply chains have friction.

So paper grows.

And when paper becomes the center of gravity, it starts shaping behavior.

When paper says silver is cheap, sellers hesitate.

When paper says silver is plentiful, buyers plan like supply is guaranteed.

When paper says everything is contained, the public stops paying attention.

Until the day the pathway from paper to metal gets tested.

Here is what that test feels like in real life.

You call.

You ask for size.

You ask for delivery.

The chart is calm. The quote sounds normal.

Then you ask the only question that matters.

"When can I have it in hand?"

A pause.

A minimum.

A lead time.

A premium that moves before price does.

A dealer who asks what size you want delivered instead of what you want exposure to.

A substitution offer.

A cash settlement suggestion.

Nothing dramatic.

Just friction.

That is the moment you realize the paper market and the physical market are not the same thing.

Paper markets feel infinite. Smooth. Continuous. Liquid.

They train everyone to relax.

But paper markets are only stable as long as most participants are willing to settle in cash.

If people accept cash settlement, paper can expand dramatically without breaking.

If people demand delivery, paper collides with inventory.

And inventory is finite.

This is why silver does not behave like a normal commodity.

It behaves like a pressure valve.

Sometimes it looks asleep.

Then it spikes like it has been held underwater.

Then it gets slammed down.

Then it tries again.

People call that volatility.

Sometimes it is.

Other times it is conflict.

The paper system pulling price down.

The physical system pulling price up.

That tug-of-war is the silver story.

And it matters because silver is a monetary metal.

Gold rising is a warning.

Silver rising is a siren.

Because rising silver tends to signal physical pressure.

And physical pressure is what breaks paper confidence.

If silver is limited, people begin to ask what else is limited.

If silver breaks out, people begin to question paper certainty.

If paper certainty weakens, institutions tighten.

If institutions tighten, liquidity shrinks.

If liquidity shrinks, the system accelerates.

To understand how explosive that test can become, we have to go deeper into the amplifier that makes paper silver possible at scale.

Leverage.

Leverage makes the room feel bigger.

Until the exit suddenly gets smaller.

CHAPTER 4

LEVERAGE, LIQUIDITY, AND THE MOMENT THE MUSIC STOPS

Leverage, Liquidity, and the Moment the Music Stops

Leverage is a magic trick.

It makes a system look stronger than it is by turning thin collateral into thick exposure.

It also explains why financial systems do not break gently.

They break abruptly.

Most people hear the word leverage and think of a mortgage or a trading account. Someone borrowing money to buy an asset.

That is leverage.

It is also the shallow end.

Real leverage is systemic.

It is embedded in how banks operate. How collateral is pledged. How derivatives multiply exposure. How market makers hedge. How futures markets function. How institutions turn liquidity into an assumption instead of a condition.

Leverage is what allows the paper metal machine to grow larger than the metal beneath it.

And the silver story cannot be understood without this.

Because silver does not live in a simple commodity market.

Silver lives inside a leveraged ecosystem that depends on predictable behavior.

It depends on contracts being rolled instead of delivered.

It depends on traders treating silver as exposure instead of substance.

It depends on participants continuing to play the same game the same way.

It depends on the music continuing.

So picture a crowded room.

A party. Music loud. People moving. It feels like there will always be more sound, more motion.

Now imagine the DJ quietly unplugs one speaker.

Most people do not notice. The room is still loud.

Then another speaker goes.

Still loud enough.

Then a few more.

Eventually the bass disappears. The sound thins. The energy shifts. The room starts to feel wrong.

Liquidity is the bass line of the system. You don't notice it until it drops out, and then everything sounds wrong.

When liquidity is thick, pressure is absorbed. Large orders move quietly. Panic disperses across many participants. Volatility stays contained.

When liquidity thins, everything changes.

Small orders move price more than they should.

Spreads widen.

Markets gap.

Prices stop feeling like measurements and start feeling like guesses.

Here is the critical point.

Leverage makes liquidity feel permanent.

Until it suddenly is not.

Leveraged systems do not merely use liquidity.

They depend on it.

They are built on the assumption that there will always be a buyer, always be a seller, always be a market maker, always be a way out.

That assumption holds.

Until it does not.

This is why silver can appear calm for long periods and then turn violent.

Not because the metal is emotional.

Because the structure around it is.

Leverage creates fragility.

And fragility reveals itself in silver faster than in many other markets because silver is smaller and more sensitive. It has less room to absorb stress. Less room to hide imbalance.

Leverage in silver shows up first through futures.

Futures contracts allow traders to control large amounts of silver exposure with relatively little capital. Margin buys access. Price movement settles most positions. Physical delivery remains the exception.

But the deeper layer is where leverage becomes a machine.

Those contracts are hedged, offset, arbitraged, and used as collateral. They sit inside strategies that span rates, currencies, mining equities, ETFs, options, and broader liquidity conditions.

Silver is not only traded as silver.

It is used as a tool inside a wider financial engine.

And engines run on two fuels.

Confidence.

Liquidity.

When both are abundant, the engine can run smoothly even when it is over-leveraged.

When either weakens, the engine misfires.

When both weaken at once, the engine seizes.

This is the core distinction.

Exposure versus delivery.

That is when the music stops. Not because the price changes.

Because the system is being asked to perform the thing it has been simulating.

In a leverage-heavy paper system, most participants want exposure. It is easier. Faster. Scalable.

But when confidence weakens, a growing number want delivery.

They want the real thing.

Not the promise.

Not the claim.

Not the paper version.

They want the bar.

Silver does not need to explode for the signal to matter.

It only needs to stop behaving like a normal market.

Liquidity only needs to thin.

Leverage only needs to get uncomfortable.

Confidence only needs to wobble.

Then physical demand meets a paper structure built on expansion.

And expansion meets limits.

Constraint.

Constraint is the enemy of leverage.

Because leverage assumes the room can always get bigger.

Silver is where the room hits the walls.

Silver is where leverage meets physics.

CHAPTER 5

THE BOND BATTLEFIELD

If you want to understand why everything feels unstable right now, stop staring at the stock market like it is the control panel.

Watch the bond market.

Stocks are loud. Stocks are emotional. Stocks are where the public vents its hopes and fears in real time. Stocks are the mood ring of a nation that checks its reflection every five minutes.

Bonds are quieter.

Bonds are where the plumbing lives.

Bonds are the spine of the system.

And when the spine starts to bend, everything above it starts compensating. To the untrained eye it looks like chaos, even though it is often adaptation.

Most people think bonds are boring for a simple reason.

They are supposed to be.

Bonds are supposed to represent safety. Predictable income. Low drama. The financial equivalent of a steady heartbeat. You lend money, you get paid interest, and at the end you get your principal back.

Clean.

But in a debt-based system, bonds are not just investments.

They are collateral.

They are the base layer of trust modern finance is built on. They sit underneath repo markets, derivatives, and global settlement. They are the high-grade paper institutions use to prove they are solid, even when everything above them is leveraged to the sky.

So the bond market is not a side story.

It is the foundation.

And that is why the bond market has become a battlefield.

In a world that runs on debt, the bond market is where promises become measurable.

Yield is the cost of trust.

When trust is thick, yields stay low.

When trust thins, yields rise.

When yields rise, consequences ripple upward through everything.

This is where the public gets lost.

They hear "yields are rising" and it sounds academic, something that belongs to economists and talking heads.

In a debt-heavy world, rising yields are not a headline.

They are a warning light.

They are the system saying the price of confidence is going up.

Think of bonds as the interest rate on reality.

When reality starts charging more, it is because someone somewhere is starting to doubt the promises.

Now here is the paradox that makes this dangerous.

The entire financial system depends on bonds being stable collateral.

But the system also depends on debt expanding.

And debt expansion eventually pressures bond stability.

That is the trap.

A debt-based system has to keep issuing more debt to keep itself moving. That debt has to be absorbed by someone. Domestic buyers. Foreign buyers. Institutions. Pension funds. Central banks.

Demand has to exist.

Because if demand weakens, yields rise.

And once yields rise, everything gets more expensive.

Government interest costs rise.

Corporate refinancing costs rise.

Mortgage rates rise.

Credit card rates rise.

Real estate slows.

Risk appetite fades.

Liquidity tightens.

Then the system does what it always does under pressure.

It reaches for intervention.

Intervention keeps the machine running.

It also teaches the public something they can feel even if they cannot explain it.

The system is no longer self-stabilizing.

It is being stabilized.

That difference matters.

Because once people sense stabilization, they start changing behavior.

And behavior is the one thing a paper system cannot fully command.

This is why the bond market matters more than the stock market in late-cycle regimes.

Stocks can float on optimism, buybacks, and narrative.

Bonds cannot.

Bonds price the cost of carrying the civilization's promises.

And right now those promises are heavy.

Debt has expanded.

Deficits have been normalized.

Political incentives reward spending.

Markets have grown dependent on central banks stepping in when pain becomes public.

In a world like that, bonds stop being boring.

They become political.

They become geopolitical.

They become legitimacy.

Because collateral is power.

Settlement infrastructure is power.

For decades, the world lived inside a strange but effective arrangement.

The dollar was the reserve currency.

U.S. debt became the reserve collateral.

Other nations held that debt as reserves.

Trade settled through dollar rails.

And the world largely agreed, implicitly, that U.S. collateral was the safest paper on Earth.

That arrangement created stability.

It also created dependency.

If the world depends on U.S. collateral, the world depends on U.S. policy.

If the world depends on U.S. settlement rails, the world depends on U.S. infrastructure.

If the world depends on the dollar, the world depends on U.S. credibility.

But the landscape has shifted.

Debt has expanded. Rivalries have intensified. Trade relationships have frayed. Nations are diversifying, not because they want chaos, but because they want options.

This is why central banks have been buying gold in size.

Not because they discovered it.

Because they understand something older than any policy regime.

Gold sits outside the promise machine.

Gold cannot be created with a keystroke.

Gold does not depend on a counterparty.

Gold is what you accumulate when you want to reduce dependence on someone else's paper.

And when gold is moving quietly into official hands, you can assume the bond battlefield is heating up even if the headlines stay calm.

At that point the story stops being finance.

It becomes strategy.

When nations diversify reserves, they are not making a trade.

They are repositioning power.

They are saying we do not want all our safety anchored to your promises.

They are saying if trust thins, we want alternatives.

That is not ideology.

That is survival.

Now zoom back in.

What does any of this have to do with silver?

Everything.

Because when bonds wobble, the collateral stack becomes fragile.

And when the collateral stack becomes fragile, the system starts searching for stability.

Hard collateral becomes magnetic.

Not because people suddenly become obsessed with metals.

Because the math starts showing through.

Because yields reveal the cost of trust is rising.

Because inflation becomes visible in daily life.

Because deficits become permanent rather than temporary.

Because the solutions increasingly require more paper, more intervention, and more managed perception.

This is why silver matters in the bond battlefield era.

Silver is the canary because it is one of the few assets that can force the system to confront reality faster than narrative can manage it.

When bonds wobble, the system tightens.

When the system tightens, hard collateral starts pulling.

When hard collateral starts pulling, silver does not rise like a normal investment.

Silver rises like a signal.

A signal that trust is thinning.

A signal that the base layer is being questioned.

A signal that the system is approaching a fork.

One path is to maintain confidence by expanding support.

The other path is to let the market price reality and accept instability.

In practice, the system almost always chooses support.

But support is not free.

Support is a form of disclosure.

It tells you the machine needs help.

And once enough people sense the machine needs help, questions spread.

When questions spread, behavior shifts.

More people seek hard collateral.

More people seek alternatives.

More people seek proof.

This is how a bond story becomes a silver story.

And it is also how a silver story becomes something bigger.

Because when bonds are the backbone and silver is the canary, the next question becomes unavoidable.

If the backbone is straining, what does the system do next?

It upgrades.

It installs new rails.

It changes how value moves.

Not because it loves innovation.

Because it needs continuity.

That is where we go next.
Because the bond battlefield is not the end of the story.
It is the pressure that forces the next system to be built.
Inflation is not a number.
It is the slow theft of certainty.

CHAPTER 6
INFLATION IS A STORY YOU LIVE INSIDE

I used to think inflation was a number.

A statistic.

A chart economists debated while the rest of us got on with our lives.

Then I watched it become a feeling.

If you want to know when inflation turns from an academic topic into lived reality, it is not when the headlines announce it. It is when ordinary people start adjusting their behavior without talking about it.

It is the moment someone stops buying their usual brand of coffee and does not even mention it.

It is the moment a family quietly switches from eating out on Fridays to making something at home, not because they suddenly became healthier, but because the math in their head changed.

It is when a contractor starts quoting jobs with bigger buffers, not because he is greedy, but because he has been burned twice and he cannot afford to be burned again.

It is when your grocery cart feels lighter and costs more anyway.

Inflation is more than an increase in prices.

Inflation is a slow-motion rewrite of what your money means.

And once that rewrite begins, it does not just hit your wallet. It reshapes the way you see the future.

Because money is time.

Money is stored effort.

Money is the promise that if you work today, your work will still carry weight tomorrow.

Inflation is what happens when that promise starts weakening.

Not all at once.

At first it is subtle. You rationalize it. You call it temporary. You blame supply chains. You blame weather. You blame greedy companies. You blame anything that makes it feel local instead of systemic.

Then it spreads.

It shows up everywhere.

And at some point you stop blaming and start adapting.

That is when inflation becomes cultural.

And once inflation becomes cultural, it becomes dangerous for a paper system.

Paper systems depend on confidence. Confidence depends on the belief that money is stable enough to plan around.

Inflation is the enemy of planning.

It turns every future decision into a guess. It makes people feel like they are running on a treadmill that speeds up without warning.

And when people feel that long enough, they start looking for anchors.

That search for anchors is one of the most powerful forces in modern finance. It is also one of the least understood.

Most people assume the public moves into hard assets because they are smart.

That is not usually the reason.

People move into hard assets because they feel disrespected by the system.

They feel their effort is being diluted.

They feel they are working harder for less.

They feel the rules are changing without their consent.

And when enough people feel that, they do not just complain.

They reposition.

They start storing value in things that do not feel like promises.

This is why inflation pushes people toward metals.

Not because metals are glamorous.

Because metals are simple.

Metal does not care who is in office.

Metal does not care what policy gets passed.

Metal is not created with a keystroke.

Metal does not require permission.

It just sits there, holding its nature.

And that nature becomes attractive when the nature of currency starts feeling unstable.

Now here is the part that makes people uncomfortable.

Inflation is not only something that happens.

Inflation is also something that gets explained.

And the explanation is always political.

Because inflation creates losers, and losers demand answers.

So a narrative gets built.

The narrative usually tries to do three things at once.

Minimize the problem.

Assign blame to something external.

Reassure the public that the system is still under control.

That narrative can work for a while.

Until daily life contradicts it.

Because daily life is the ultimate fact-checker.

A press conference can say inflation is improving, but if your insurance premium jumps again, you do not feel improvement.

A report can say core inflation is stabilizing, but if rent climbs, groceries rise, and repairs cost more, you do not feel stabilization.

This is how inflation erodes trust.

Not through numbers.

Through contradiction.

Inflation is the moment the official story and the lived story diverge.

And when the official story diverges from lived reality, people start looking for alternate stories that match what they are experiencing.

That is when you see the cultural shift.

More people talking about hard assets.

More people asking what sound money even means.

More people questioning whether the system is designed to protect them or extract from them.

And there is a deeper layer.

Inflation is not only money losing value.

Inflation is the system revealing its priorities.

When inflation rises, the question becomes simple.

Who gets protected?

Not everyone experiences inflation the same way.

People with assets often get protected. Stocks can rise. Real estate can rise. Businesses can raise prices. People with leverage can benefit because they repay debt with cheaper dollars.

But the person living paycheck to paycheck has no hedge.

They do not own the assets that inflate.

They own the currency that dilutes.

So inflation becomes a transfer.

A slow transfer of purchasing power from the saver to the debtor, from the wage earner to the asset holder, from the person who plays by the rules to the person who understands the loopholes.

This is why inflation creates anger that feels bigger than economics.

It feels like injustice.

And injustice changes behavior.

Now bring it back to silver, because silver sits right in the crosswind of inflation psychology.

Gold is the traditional hedge. The one central banks respect. The one institutions default to.

Silver is the renegade.

Silver is what the public reaches for when they want hard money but gold feels out of reach. Silver is what everyday people buy when they want something real in their hands.

Silver is the working man's monetary metal.

But that is only half the story.

The other half is what makes silver uniquely explosive in inflation cycles.

Silver is also pulled by industry.

Inflation does not only push investors toward silver.

Inflation can coincide with industrial expansion, energy buildouts, technology shifts, and infrastructure demand.

When those forces align, something rare happens.

Investment demand and industrial demand pull on the same finite supply.

That is when silver stops behaving like a normal market.

That is when silver becomes a stress test.

Because paper can absorb investor demand for a while by expanding claims.

But industry cannot run on claims.

Factories cannot solder with promises.

Solar panels cannot conduct with paper contracts.

Electronics cannot be manufactured with exposure.

Industry needs metal.

So when inflation pushes the public toward physical silver while industrial demand stays strong, the paper system starts feeling pressure.

Not the kind of pressure that shows up in a polite chart.

The kind that shows up in availability.

Premiums.

Delivery timelines.

Inventory drawdowns.

Procurement teams scrambling, not to speculate, but to keep production running.

This is where the silver story becomes more than a price story.

It becomes a supply story.

And supply stories break paper narratives.

Because in a paper world, the system can always create more claims.

In a physical world, the system has to confront limits.

Inflation accelerates that confrontation because it makes the public more sensitive to the idea of limits.

Inflation is the moment people remember real things matter.

Food matters.

Energy matters.

Housing matters.

Materials matter.

And when people start thinking in real things, silver starts shining differently.

Silver feels real.

It has weight.

It has texture.

It has a sound when you drop it on wood.

It turns the abstract physical.

That matters psychologically.

In an inflationary environment, psychology is half the market.

Now pause here, because most books miss what inflation is really doing.

Inflation is not the end of the story.

Inflation is the warning that the system is choosing a path.

Once inflation becomes persistent, policymakers face an ugly menu.

They can tighten. Raise rates. Reduce demand. Try to restore currency confidence.

But tightening breaks things.

It breaks over-leveraged markets.

It breaks refinancing cycles.

It breaks budget math.

It breaks the illusion that debt can expand forever without consequence.

Or they can support.

They can print. Stimulate. Backstop. Smooth. Choose stability today at the cost of currency confidence tomorrow.

Most modern systems choose support.

Not because they love it.

Because the alternative is politically and socially painful.

Which means inflation is not merely a surprise.

It is often an outcome.

An outcome of choosing stability now over stability later.

And when enough people understand that, demand for hard assets stops being fear.

It becomes logic.

That is when silver becomes a serious conversation.

A strategic conversation.

Because currency stability is not guaranteed by good intentions.

It is guaranteed by discipline.

And discipline becomes rare when debt is high and incentives are political.

This is the tension that defines our era.

A world that wants stability.

A system that requires expansion.

A public that feels the cost.

Hard assets that become increasingly attractive because they exist outside the paper story.

That is why inflation matters.

And it is why silver's role is changing.

Because in an inflationary world, silver stops being just a metal.

It becomes a message.

A message that the public is starting to feel something fundamental.

The story of money is changing.

And when the story changes, markets move.

Next, we take this understanding and push into the next layer.

Because inflation is not only what happens to prices.

Inflation is what happens to behavior.

And behavior is what breaks systems when it reaches a threshold.

That threshold is where silver stops whispering and starts forcing a reckoning.

The market does not wait for truth. It moves the moment belief changes.

CHAPTER 7

WHEN BEHAVIOR TURNS, EVERYTHING REPRICES

There is a point in every financial cycle where math stops being the main driver.

Behavior takes over.

Logical people hate that idea because it sounds like superstition. Like psychology replacing fundamentals. Like crowds and emotion overpowering reality.

But behavior is not the opposite of fundamentals.

Behavior is fundamentals becoming visible.

It is the moment the public stops treating a problem like a headline and starts treating it like a condition.

It is the moment people stop debating and start adjusting.

And once that happens, repricing begins. Not because someone announced it, but because a critical mass quietly agreed the world is different now.

You can see the turn in small moments long before it shows up in public narratives.

A store manager orders extra inventory just in case.

A business owner raises prices faster than usual because future costs feel uncertain.

A family keeps more cash on hand because systems feel less dependable.

A friend who never cared about money suddenly asks, “Do you think we’re okay?”

That is behavior turning.

And when behavior turns, paper systems start to feel exposed.

Because paper systems rely on one invisible pillar more than any other.

Normalcy.

Normalcy is the assumption that things will continue.

That the store will restock.

That the bank will clear.

That the currency will hold.

That supply chains will behave.

That government will manage.

That tomorrow will look roughly like yesterday.

Normalcy is why people accept abstractions.

It is why paper claims can trade as if they are the thing.

It is why a digital balance can feel safe enough to sleep on.

It is why people can make plans five years out.

Normalcy is the oxygen that keeps the paper world breathing.

So when normalcy thins, people begin craving proof.

Not proof in the philosophical sense.

Proof in the physical sense.

Proof you can hold.

Proof you can withdraw.

Proof you can move without permission.

Proof that does not depend on a counterparty staying solvent or a system staying calm.

This is where silver becomes uniquely important.

Silver sits right at the edge of proof.

It is affordable enough for ordinary people to buy.

Recognizable enough to feel legitimate.

Physical enough to satisfy the itch for reality.

Connected enough to industry that it does not behave like a purely emotional hedge.

Silver is one of the first places the public goes when behavior turns.

That is not theory.

That is pattern.

In calm times, silver feels like a hobby.

In tense times, silver feels like a life raft.

But the public is not the only force that matters.

Behavior turns at the institutional level too, and when institutions turn, the system can move in a way that feels sudden and violent.

Institutions do not panic on television.

They reposition quietly.

They shorten duration.

They hedge differently.

They reduce risk exposure.

They change collateral preferences.

They move from "we believe" to "we verify."

And because institutions operate at scale, subtle shifts create major ripples.

This is where the story becomes mechanical.

In a leveraged system, behavior changes do not only move prices.

They change liquidity.

They change collateral availability.

They change market-making.

They change spreads.

They change the system's ability to absorb stress.

In other words, behavior changes do not only create demand.

They create fragility.

This is why things can feel stable for a long time and then suddenly become unstable all at once.

The instability did not appear overnight.

It accumulated.

Then behavior crossed a threshold.

And once behavior crosses a threshold, repricing is fast.

Think of a crowd leaving a stadium.

One person stands up.

Then another.

Then a section.

Then a wave.

At first the exits are fine.

Then bottlenecks form.

Then people feel the bottleneck.

Then urgency spreads.

Then you get crowd motion.

Not because everyone became irrational, but because everyone sensed the same constraint at the same time.

That is what happens in financial repricings.

It is not always fear.

It is often constraint recognition.

And silver is one of the best constraint detectors in the system because it is both monetary and physical.

When behavior turns toward delivery, silver tells the truth.

When behavior turns toward proof, silver tells the truth.

When behavior turns toward hard collateral, silver tells the truth.

And the truth is rarely comfortable for a system built on paper claims.

This is where we have to use a word most people avoid.

Shortage.

In the physical world, shortage is simple. If there is not enough of something, price rises until demand cools or supply expands.

In the paper world, shortage is complicated, because paper can simulate abundance.

Paper can manufacture the feeling of supply by manufacturing claims.

Paper can keep prices lower than physical reality would demand by expanding the tradeable silver universe without requiring delivery.

That works as long as behavior stays cooperative.

As long as most participants accept cash settlement.

As long as most participants want exposure instead of metal.

As long as most participants stay inside normalcy.

But when behavior changes, cooperation gets tested.

Because the paper machine can create claims.

It cannot create bars.

Which is why the most critical moment in the silver story is rarely the price spike.

It is the moment the market begins splitting into two realities.

The paper price and the physical price.

When those two start diverging, the canary is singing loud enough that even people who do not watch silver start hearing it.

That divergence shows up in three places.

First, premiums.

When you walk into a shop, you are not paying spot.

You are paying spot plus premium.

In calm times, the premium is tolerable and boring.

In stressed times, the premium becomes a message.

It tells you the physical market is tighter than the paper market admits.

Second, availability.

It is not only that premiums rise.

It is that product disappears.

Not permanently. Not everywhere.

But enough to plant a new thought in the buyer's mind.

Maybe I should buy now because later might be harder.

That thought spreads fast.

Third, delivery timelines.

When industrial buyers begin worrying about supply, they do not wait.

They lock contracts.

Secure relationships.

Prioritize procurement.

Become less price-sensitive and more supply-sensitive.

And once industry becomes supply-sensitive, the entire silver market shifts.

Speculative demand can fade quickly.

Industrial demand is stubborn.

Industry needs what it needs.

If industry is bidding for supply while the public is stacking physical, the paper system starts facing a real question.

How much of this paper silver can actually become physical if behavior changes further?

That question is where repricing begins.

Not the repricing of silver alone.

The repricing of confidence.

Because if silver reveals that paper claims exceed physical reality by an uncomfortable margin, the public starts asking a bigger question.

If they can do it in silver, what else can they do it in?

Currency.

Bonds.

The collateral stack.

The safety story.

This is why silver is not just a trade.

Silver is a psychological lever on the fiat narrative.

When silver is sleepy, fiat confidence looks stable.

When silver becomes restless, fiat confidence starts getting questioned.

And when fiat confidence gets questioned, behavior shifts again.

That is the feedback loop.

That is why silver cycles can accelerate in a way that shocks people.

The move is not just about metal.

It is about trust leaving paper.

Now add the layer most people ignore until it hits them directly.

Government behavior.

Governments are not passive observers.

They are participants with incentives, tools, and survival instincts.

When behavior shifts at the public level, governments tend to respond in ways that reveal what they value most.

Control.

Continuity.

Confidence.

That response can show up as policy shifts, messaging shifts, liquidity interventions, regulatory changes, or narrative management.

But one reality does not change.

Governments cannot print physical silver.

They can influence price.

They can influence markets.

They can influence perception.

They cannot manufacture supply.

Which means that if silver becomes a constraint in an era increasingly dependent on electrification, technology, and infrastructure, the metal becomes strategically important.

Not because it is shiny.

Because it is necessary.

And necessity is what turns economics into geopolitics.

So what happens when behavior turns?

People seek proof.

Physical demand rises.

Shortages appear at the edges.

Premiums rise and inventories tighten.

Institutions hedge differently.

Liquidity thins.

The paper machine gets tested.

The narrative begins cracking.

And once the narrative cracks, behavior accelerates further.

That is the chain.

That is the cycle.

That is why the most important thing to watch in silver is not the chart.

It is behavior.

The behavior of buyers.

The behavior of industrial users.

The behavior of institutions.

The behavior of policymakers.

Because the moment behavior crosses a threshold, repricing stops being theoretical.

It becomes inevitable.

Next, we step into the part of the story most people only half understand.

Supply.

Not the simplified version.

The real version.

The bottlenecks, the hidden constraints, and the reason silver supply is far less flexible than the paper system wants you to believe.

Because once you see supply reality, the silver canary stops feeling like a metaphor and starts feeling like a clock.

Paper can fake abundance. Physical reality always collects the payment.

CHAPTER 8

SUPPLY IS THE TRICK BEHIND THE TRICK

There is a moment in every great illusion when the audience starts leaning forward.

They do not know exactly what is wrong yet, but they can feel it.

Something does not match.

The smile is a little too wide. The trick takes a beat too long. The hand moves slightly out of rhythm. And the crowd, even if it cannot explain it, starts sensing that the performance depends on them staying polite.

Silver is like that.

For a long time, the paper market has been the stage. Lights, music, pricing, confidence. And most people have played their role perfectly. They have traded the story of silver instead of the substance. They have treated paper as the reference point. They have watched spot like it was truth.

But the real story has never been spot.

The real story is supply.

Not the simplified version. Not the spreadsheet version. The real-world version. Messy. Stubborn. Late. More expensive than expected. Refusing to scale on demand just because finance wants it to.

Because there is one problem paper cannot solve.

You can print claims.

You cannot print atoms.

And when you look closely, silver supply is not built for a world that suddenly needs more of it.

Most people imagine supply works like this.

Price goes up. Miners mine more. Supply increases. Everything balances.

That is the classroom version.

The version that makes the system feel self-correcting.

Real supply does not respond like that, especially with silver.

Silver supply moves slowly.

Silver supply is tied to other metals.

Silver supply is constrained by decisions made years earlier.

Silver supply is limited by refining capacity, energy costs, labor realities, permitting delays, environmental rules, geopolitics, transportation friction, and the simple fact that the Earth does not care what price you want.

And the deeper you go, the more you find a fact that should make every investor sit up straighter.

Silver is not primarily mined for silver.

A large percentage of global silver arrives as a byproduct of mining other metals, especially lead, zinc, copper, and gold. Which means silver production is often a passenger, not the driver.

So even if silver's price rises, it does not automatically trigger a silver mining boom.

If lead and zinc production slows, silver supply can tighten even while silver is screaming higher on a chart.

If copper demand shifts, silver output shifts.

If a major base metal mine closes, silver supply takes collateral damage.

Silver is chained to the economics of other markets.

That makes its supply less responsive and more fragile than most people assume.

Now picture the conflict this creates.

Imagine you are a factory that needs silver for components.

You do not care that silver is up this year.

You care whether silver is available.

Now imagine the world entering an era of accelerating electrification, advanced electronics, solar buildouts, defense systems, and medical applications.

Silver is not optional in many of those uses.

It is not a luxury input.

It is a performance input.

That means industrial demand is not only growing.

It is becoming structural.

And structural demand collides with inelastic supply.

When inelastic supply meets rising demand, price does not move politely.

It moves in steps.

It moves in gaps.

It moves in ruptures.

This is why silver rallies often look like ambushes.

Not because the market is insane.

Because the market is waking up to physical constraint.

Now add the second supply reality most people misunderstand.

Above-ground inventories.

People talk about inventory like it is one big vault the world can open if needed.

It is not.

Inventory is fragmented. Distributed. Often already spoken for. And much of it is sitting in forms that are not economically easy to retrieve.

Silver in electronics is not sitting neatly in a warehouse.

Silver in solar panels is not waiting in a stack to be reclaimed.

Silver in industrial components is not a pile of bars you can scoop up.

It is embedded.

Dispersed.

Inside devices.

Which means when demand rises, you cannot simply "use the inventory."

You have to mine.

You have to refine.

You have to source.

And those processes take time.

Time is the variable paper markets underestimate most.

Paper moves at the speed of thought.

Physical moves at the speed of reality.

Mining is slow.

Permitting is slow.

Building new production is slow.

Even restarting old production is slow.

In a world used to solving problems by creating more paper, that slowness becomes a pressure amplifier.

Because paper markets do not like waiting.

They like liquidity.

They like immediate fulfillment.

They like the illusion of infinite supply.

Physical silver does not care what markets prefer.

It only cares what exists and what can be produced.

Which brings us to the third constraint.

Refining.

Silver does not show up as a finished product the moment it comes out of the ground. It moves through a chain. Ore is extracted, processed, refined, fabricated, shipped, distributed.

Every step has bottlenecks.

Every step has cost pressure.

Every step has friction.

Friction matters most when demand accelerates.

Because demand can surge in weeks.

Supply cannot.

When demand surges in a market that cannot scale supply quickly, something else happens.

People begin competing for priority.

Industry locks contracts.

Wholesalers control distribution.

Mints ration.

Premiums rise.

Delivery delays appear.

And the public learns the difference between price and availability.

People do not learn about physical constraints by staring at a chart.

They learn the way people learn about bank stability.

They learn when they try to withdraw.

Silver has a similar moment.

You do not learn the supply chain is tight from an article.

You learn when you try to buy and cannot.

Or when you can buy, but at a price that tells you the paper number is a suggestion, not a reality.

That is when the canary becomes impossible to ignore.

And here is what makes silver uniquely volatile.

The physical distribution system is not built for a sudden surge in mass retail demand.

If millions of people decided they wanted a meaningful amount of physical silver, the system would not smoothly adjust.

It would strain.

Because it was designed for steady flow, not a public rush.

Most people say, "There is plenty of silver out there."

What they usually mean is there is plenty of paper silver.

Plenty of exposure.

Plenty of claims.

Physical silver is a different world.

Physical silver has limits.

And those limits rarely announce themselves with fireworks.

They introduce themselves in whispers.

A dealer says, "We are out of Eagles."

A wholesaler says, "We can get it, but it will take a few weeks."

A premium quietly jumps.

A mint pauses production.

A buyer gets told, "If you want it, lock it now."

That is how constraints enter the room.

That is how the air starts changing.

And once the air changes, the market does not need everyone to notice.

It only needs enough people to notice.

Because once enough people act on constraint awareness, behavior shifts again.

People begin preempting scarcity.

They begin buying ahead.

They begin stacking.

They begin securing supply while it is still available.

That behavior becomes its own force.

A force paper cannot fully counter, because paper cannot deliver what does not exist.

This part of the silver story feels small until it suddenly is not.

Because markets do not change when everyone agrees.

They change when the marginal buyer changes behavior.

They change when new demand shows up at the edges and grows faster than supply can respond.

And silver is a market where edges matter.

It is small compared to other asset classes.

Easier to move.

Easier to stress.

Easier to tighten.

Which means once physical constraints become visible, repricing can be sharp.

Not because the world has gone insane.

Because the world has bumped into the physical boundary of a system that has been living comfortably in paper.

This is why silver is not only a story about investing.

It is a story about limits.

It is a story about how modern finance tries to abstract reality until reality refuses to cooperate.

And silver is one of the first places where reality tends to refuse.

Now we have built the foundation.

Paper.

Leverage.

Bonds.

Inflation and behavior.

Supply and why it cannot flex the way paper wants.

So the next logical question is the one the system hopes most people never ask.

If physical silver is constrained and paper claims are large, what happens when demand for physical becomes strategic?

Not retail demand.

Not speculation.

Strategic demand.

The kind that comes from governments. From industries that cannot fail. From nations that want supply security. From institutions that do not care about paying up if it means owning what they need.

That is where this stops being a market story and becomes a power story.

That is where we go next.

When nations want metal, they do not announce it. They absorb it.

CHAPTER 9

STRATEGIC DEMAND

Most people imagine "resource wars" as something that happens with oil.

Pipelines. Tankers. Sanctions. Soldiers. Headlines.

Silver does not get that mythology, which is ironic, because silver is quietly becoming one of the most strategic materials on Earth.

Not because it is shiny.

Because it is embedded.

Silver sits inside the modern world the way wiring sits inside a wall. You do not think about it until the lights go out. And by then, pretending it was optional becomes a luxury you cannot afford.

That is what is changing now.

We are moving into an era where raw materials are not only commodities.

They are leverage.

They are national security.

They are industrial survival.

And when a material becomes essential to civilian infrastructure and defense capability, it stops being just a market.

It becomes a strategic priority.

Strategic priorities do not behave like normal buyers.

A normal buyer cares about price.

A strategic buyer cares about certainty.

If you have never watched procurement at scale, it is hard to grasp how different those mindsets are.

A normal buyer looks at a chart.

A strategic buyer looks at the future and asks one question.

What happens to us if we do not have this?

That question changes everything.

Once a material crosses into that category, the market begins shifting in subtle but powerful ways.

It starts with stockpiles.

Not the dramatic kind announced on television.

The quiet kind.

A ministry signs contracts.

A manufacturer locks in multi-year supply.

A defense contractor over-orders under the umbrella of redundancy.

Inventories rise without explanation.

Strategic demand rarely shows up as a headline at first.

It shows up as missing product.

It shows up as tightening supply nobody can fully account for.

It shows up as a market that behaves differently than the paper price suggests it should.

It shows up as sudden competition for delivery.

And it shows up as behavior that looks irrational if you think the buyer is trying to win a trade.

But the buyer is not trying to win a trade.

They are trying to avoid a future failure.

That is strategic demand.

It is buying from the future.

Now look at where the world is headed.

Electrification.

Automation.

Artificial intelligence infrastructure.

Energy buildouts.

Solar.

Grid upgrades.

Advanced electronics.

Defense modernization.

Layered on top of all of that is rising geopolitical friction.

You do not have to be pessimistic to see the shape of it.

You just have to be honest.

The world is less unified than it used to be.

Supply chains are less trusted than they used to be.

The assumption that you can always buy what you need on the open market is becoming less safe.

That is the environment where strategic materials become king.

And silver sits near the center of that future.

Here is the key.

Strategic buyers do not buy the way retail buyers do.

Retail demand is cyclical. It surges when fear rises and fades when fear calms. It is emotional. It is news-driven. It can be powerful, but it is inconsistent.

Strategic demand is different.

Strategic demand is slow, persistent, and sticky.

Once an institution decides a material matters, it does not undecide easily.

If a country decides it needs secure supply, it does not sell back its stockpile because the chart went sideways.

If a defense program requires consistent material availability, it does not accept "sorry, we are out."

If an industrial buildout is planned for a decade, it does not gamble on short-term market convenience.

Strategic demand is like gravity.

Quiet at first.

Then undeniable.

This is where the silver story becomes more serious than most investors realize.

Because the silver market is not massive.

It does not have the depth of crude oil.

It does not have the liquidity of major currencies.

It does not have the scale of U.S. Treasuries.

Silver is relatively small.

Which means strategic demand can stress it faster than people expect.

A few large, determined buyers can change the landscape.

Not by bidding the price up dramatically on day one.

By consistently removing supply from the available ecosystem.

By prioritizing physical over paper.

By securing contracts that reduce the float.

By changing the behavior of wholesalers, refiners, and fabricators.

By turning the market into a funnel.

This is where a strange process begins.

You can call it nationalization, but it rarely looks like a government marching into a mine.

It looks like supply becoming politically sensitive.

Export restrictions.

Strategic reserve policies.

Industrial prioritization.

Preferential contracts.

Quiet agreements.

All of it happening beneath the surface while the public still thinks silver is a sleepy commodity.

The word nationalization is heavy, so let me be precise.

We are moving toward a reality where strategic materials are increasingly treated like protected assets.

Managed.

Influenced.

Secured.

Because the alternative is dependence.

And dependence is vulnerability.

Once a nation realizes it depends on another nation for a key input, it starts planning how to reduce that dependence.

That is one reason you see supply chains being reshored, diversified, and politicized.

It is not only about jobs.

It is about control.

And control is where markets become less free.

If a country believes silver is essential to its infrastructure and defense, it will not leave silver entirely to a free market if that market threatens continuity.

That is statecraft.

The state does not prioritize efficient price discovery.

The state prioritizes survival.

Now picture what happens when multiple nations reach that conclusion at the same time.

They do not announce it.

They act.

They stockpile.

They secure contracts.

They invest in mining and refining.

They create incentives.

They restrict exports when necessary.

As this happens, the silver market develops a new character.

Less elastic.

Less tolerant of spikes.

More sensitive to disruption.

Easier to stress.

Because more of the available supply is already spoken for.

This is when silver starts behaving like a strategic metal, not a commodity.

And when a commodity becomes strategic, price discovery changes.

Price is no longer shaped only by profit motives.

It is shaped by power motives.

Security motives.

Continuity motives.

And those motives do not fade when the chart looks tired.

They persist.

Now here is the part most investors miss because it is counterintuitive.

Strategic demand does not always show up as a rising price immediately.

Sometimes it shows up as suppressed volatility.

Because strategic buyers often prefer stability, quiet accumulation, predictable inputs, and minimal signaling.

So instead of bidding the price up, they remove supply quietly.

They let paper markets keep the lid on the narrative.

They allow the public to stay asleep.

Until the public wakes up on its own.

And once the public wakes up, the strategic advantage is already secured.

That is how serious players accumulate.

They do not buy when the crowd is screaming.

They buy when the crowd is distracted.

That is why silver is a canary.

Silver does not only signal monetary stress.

Silver signals strategic stress.

It signals when the world is beginning to compete for the same real inputs.

And when competition rises, the soft assumptions of free markets begin to erode.

This is why silver is not only a hedge.

It is a narrative fracture point.

Because if silver becomes visibly strategic, the public starts asking questions that reach beyond silver.

Why does this material matter?

How much exists?

Who controls it?

Why does the paper price not match the physical struggle?

Why is availability becoming the story?

Those questions spread.

And repricing is not only about scarcity.

It is about awareness of scarcity.

Awareness spreads faster than supply can respond.

So we are entering a stage of the silver story where the key variable is not what retail investors believe.

It is what strategic actors are doing quietly.

What industries are locking in.

What governments are prioritizing.

What supply chains are being rebuilt around.

Because once silver is treated as strategic, it stops being just a metal.

It becomes part of national policy, industrial policy, and security policy.

And that pulls the market into a new era.

An era where old paper mechanisms strain harder.

An era where physical gets bid for first.

An era where the gap between claims and reality becomes more dangerous.

Now we add the final layer.

Strategic competition does not only affect supply.

It affects trust.

It affects settlement.

It affects rails.

When nations compete, they do not only compete for materials.

They compete for the systems that settle trade.

And when that competition intensifies, the world starts building alternatives to the old reserve model.

That is where we go next.

New technology changes the rails. It does not change the laws.

CHAPTER 10

NEW RAILS, SAME LAWS

When a system starts straining, the first instinct is always to patch it.

Raise a ceiling here.

Lower a floor there.

Add liquidity.

Change a rule.

Rename a program.

Adjust the optics.

For a while, patching works. It buys time. It creates the appearance of continuity. It keeps people calm enough to keep playing along.

Then patching stops being enough.

At that point, systems do not only patch.

They upgrade.

They build new rails.

And they sell the rebuild as progress.

Sometimes it is progress.

Often it is survival.

That is where the global financial world is now.

Because when trust becomes expensive, settlement becomes strategic.

Put this into a picture you can hold.

Imagine a town where everyone trades with handwritten IOUs. It works because everyone knows everyone, and the system runs on social trust.

Then the town becomes a city.

People stop knowing each other. Fraud gets easier. Defaults get larger. The same IOU that once felt personal starts feeling like a liability.

So the city builds a ledger.

A registry.

A centralized way to track who owes what.

That is banking in its simplest form.

Now imagine the city becomes a nation, and the nation becomes a global network, and the IOUs go digital, and the volume becomes massive, and trust begins fraying between major players.

At some point, the ledger itself becomes a battlefield.

Who controls it?

Who gets access?

Who can be cut off?

Who can freeze whose assets?

Who enforces the rules?

Who gets to rewrite them mid-game?

That is where we are.

And once you see it that way, a lot of "innovation" stops looking like a tech story and starts looking like strategy.

The world is building new rails because the old rails have become political.

Politics creates friction.

Friction creates cost.

Cost creates instability.

That is why the language of global finance has shifted.

More talk about alternative settlement systems.

More talk about trade in local currencies.

More talk about a multipolar monetary order.

More talk about digital currency infrastructure.

More talk about tokenized assets.

More talk about blockchain-based settlement.

On the surface, it looks like adoption.

Underneath, it is a trust problem.

And trust problems trigger one of two responses.

Either you rebuild trust.

Or you build a system that needs less of it.

New rails are the second response.

But here is what people miss.

New rails do not change the underlying truth.

They change speed.

They change visibility.

They change efficiency.

They do not change scarcity.

They do not change physics.

They do not change the fact that real value ultimately rests on real things.

You can build a faster train system and move goods quicker.

You cannot move goods you do not have.

You can build a better payment network and settle faster.

You cannot settle promises that exceed underlying reality forever.

This is why silver stays central even in a world obsessed with digital solutions.

Silver is not threatened by new rails.

Silver is revealed by them.

Because new rails accelerate everything.

They accelerate capital flight.

They accelerate repricing.

They accelerate demand surges.

They accelerate the speed at which the public moves from "I trust the system" to "I want proof."

The digital world does not remove the need for real assets.

It increases the speed at which the world can rush toward them.

If you want to understand why silver could become more volatile in a more digital future, start there.

Speed.

Now hold two realities in your mind at the same time.

The financial layer is getting faster.

Instant settlement. Faster conversion. Fewer frictions between one form of value and another.

At the same time, the physical layer is still slow.

It takes years to build a mine.

Years to expand refining.

Years to scale industrial capacity.

Years to fix a supply chain that has been optimized for efficiency instead of resilience.

So we are entering a world where finance becomes more liquid and reactive while production stays constrained and stubborn.

That gap creates tension.

Silver lives inside that tension.

Silver is monetary enough to be bought as a store of value.

Silver is industrial enough to be required as a material.

Silver is a bridge asset.

Bridge assets matter most during regime change.

And that is what this is.

A regime change.

Not only a market cycle.

A shift in how trust is distributed globally.

A shift in how settlement occurs.

A shift in how power is expressed.

A shift in what collateral means.

So when people say "digital money," the deeper question is simple.

Digital money backed by what?

Money is always backed by something.

If it is not backed by metal, it is backed by the state.

If it is not backed by the state, it is backed by network trust.

If it is not backed by trust, it is backed by force.

If it is not backed by force, it is backed by scarcity.

Every system has a foundation.

It can be obvious or hidden, but it exists.

And this is where the future story merges back into the silver story.

In a multipolar world, trust fragments.

When trust fragments, nations seek assets and systems that reduce counterparty risk.

When nations seek assets and systems that reduce counterparty risk, hard collateral becomes more important.

Hard collateral means assets you can hold, settle, or secure without depending on someone else's permission.

Gold has always been the reserve anchor for this reason.

But silver is the material anchor of modern industry.

It is the metal inside the hardware of the future.

So the world is moving toward a dual collateral reality.

Gold as reserve anchor.

Silver as industrial anchor.

New rails do not change that.

They amplify it.

They make the migration toward proof faster.

They make the gap between claims and physical reality more visible.

They make the demand for anchors more fluid.

This is why we have to be careful with the way we talk about innovation.

Innovation can be a mask.

It can distract people from the fact that the system still runs on confidence.

And confidence, once fractured, is hard to rebuild.

So the question becomes:

What happens when new rails are built in a world where confidence is thinning?

It depends on who controls the rails.

It depends on who gets access.

It depends on how rules are enforced.

It depends on whether the rails are neutral or politicized.

It depends on whether the rails expand freedom or expand control.

That is the most sensitive layer of this whole conversation.

Because the move toward new rails is not only about efficiency.

It is also about governance.

Who gets to transact.

Who gets to store wealth.

Who gets to move value across borders.

Who gets to opt out.

Every rail has gatekeepers.

Every gatekeeper creates incentives.

Every incentive shapes behavior.

Which returns us to the core truth of this book.

Behavior changes markets.

Markets reveal stress.

Silver reveals stress early.

So if we are entering an era of new rails, fragmented trust, and strategic competition for materials, silver is not only a market.

It is a signal.

A signal of how quickly the world is moving toward constraint.

A signal of how much paper confidence remains.

A signal of whether the upgrades are truly stabilizing or only buying time.

Because you can build new rails all you want.

You cannot rail your way out of scarcity.

You cannot code your way out of physics.

You cannot paper over a physical constraint forever.

Eventually the physical world speaks.

And silver is one of the first places it speaks loudly enough for everyone to hear.

Next, we go brutally practical.

What does a silver stress event look like in real life?

Not charts.

Not theory.

Dealers. Supply chains. Premiums. Cash settlement. Delivery delays. Public awareness. Institutional behavior.

Because once you can visualize that scenario clearly, you will understand why the silver canary is not a metaphor.

It is a warning system.

And it is already humming.

A real shortage does not arrive with sirens. It arrives with delays.

CHAPTER 11

WHAT A SILVER STRESS EVENT LOOKS LIKE

A silver stress event does not start with fireworks.

It starts with something small enough to dismiss.

A delay.

A higher premium.

A "temporary" shortage.

A dealer saying, "We can get it, but it'll take longer than usual."

Most people shrug because modern life trained us to accept friction. Packages show up late. Flights get rescheduled. Stores run out of random items and restock a week later. Normal.

That is why the early phase is dangerous.

It hides inside normalcy.

And normalcy is the strongest sedative on Earth.

When people picture a market breaking, they imagine a dramatic moment. A chart ripping upward, anchors panicking, the word collapse flying across the screen.

Real stress events do not introduce themselves as emergencies.

They introduce themselves as inconveniences.

That is the first lesson.

The second lesson is the one that rearranges the whole subject.

A silver stress event is not primarily about price.

It is about availability.

Price is information.

Availability is reality.

If you want to understand what happens, stop thinking like a trader and start thinking like someone trying to source something essential.

Imagine you run a factory and you need silver for production.

It is not optional.

It is not a position.

It is an input.

Without it, the line slows. Without it, deadlines slip. Without it, contracts get missed. The losses from downtime dwarf the extra dollars per ounce.

That is how real demand behaves.

Now zoom out.

Thousands of factories. Mints. Refiners. Distributors. Defense suppliers. All operating on tight schedules and just-in-time assumptions.

Now add the final ingredient.

A public increasingly aware of inflation, increasingly uneasy about currency, increasingly hungry for proof they can hold.

That is when stress becomes visible.

Not as one giant announcement.

As a stack of small signals that start adding up.

Here is what it tends to look like on the ground.

It starts in retail because retail is the most sensitive to fear.

Coin shops get picked over.

Online dealers flip to out of stock.

Backorders become normal.

Premiums rise quietly, then sharply.

And you notice something that feels impossible if you only live on charts.

Spot might not move much at all.

Spot can stay calm while the physical market is screaming.

That is the split.

Chart reality.

Try-to-buy-it reality.

Once that split becomes obvious, behavior changes.

People who were on the fence act.

People who already own silver stop selling.

Dealers tighten inventory.

Wholesalers get selective.

The market starts behaving less like a river and more like funnels.

Then the stress event moves from retail into wholesale and industrial layers.

Delivery times stretch.

Not because one supplier is slow.

Because the whole chain is under pressure.

Mints cannot produce fast enough.

Fabricators get backed up.

Refiners prioritize larger contracts.

Smaller buyers get pushed to the back of the line.

And the language changes.

You stop hearing "we can get it."

You start hearing "we might be able to get it."

That shift is subtle.

It is also everything.

Markets move on confidence.

When confidence in availability weakens, price becomes secondary.

People stop bidding for bargains and start bidding for certainty.

Now the paper system gets tested.

This is where most people misunderstand paper versus physical.

Paper does not vanish.

Paper gets busier.

Volume rises. Volatility rises. The futures market becomes a pressure valve. It offers exposure without requiring anyone to touch a bar.

In the early phase, that can work.

Paper can absorb a lot of fear by giving speculators and hedgers a place to trade.

But paper cannot absorb one thing.

A sustained demand shift toward physical.

If enough participants stop rolling contracts and start saying, "I want metal," the system has to prove it can convert paper into physical at scale.

And that is where inventory shows up.

Inventory is where constraints live.

So what does the system do?

It responds the way paper systems always respond.

It discourages the behavior that forces a reckoning.

It raises the cost of delivery.

It adds friction to delivery.

It leans on cash settlement.

It creates incentives that make participants hesitate before choosing physical.

Not always out of malice.

Out of necessity.

Leverage-heavy systems do not like being dragged into physical reality.

Physical reality does not negotiate.

Now we arrive at the moment that matters most.

The premium for certainty.

That is the moment paper stops being the reference point.

Not officially.

In practice.

If you want a human analogy, it is simple.

Think about bottled water before a storm.

On paper, the price is still $2.

In the store, shelves are half empty.

The next store is empty.

The next store has a few cases, priced like gold.

So what is the real price?

The official number?

Or the number that actually gets you water?

That is what happens in a silver stress event.

The real price becomes the price of obtaining metal.

And once that reality spreads, the chart begins catching up in violent steps.

Because the biggest money starts stepping in.

Institutions.

Funds.

Large industrial buyers.

Strategic buyers.

And they are not shopping for fair value.

They are shopping for positioning.

They are shopping for protection.

They are shopping for certainty.

They do not want to be the last ones trying to exit paper after the world starts demanding proof.

This is how stress events climb the stack.

Retail tightness becomes wholesale tightness.

Wholesale tightness becomes industrial concern.

Industrial concern becomes contract locking.

Contract locking reduces float.

Reduced float increases volatility.

Volatility draws attention.

Attention pulls in more retail demand.

More demand tightens supply further.

The cycle feeds itself.

Then comes the final accelerant.

Narrative.

Once physical tightness is obvious, the story changes.

Silver stops being boring.

It becomes interesting.

It becomes social.

Podcasts. Channels. Media segments. Friends texting friends.

Are you seeing this?

That is when the public stops viewing silver as a commodity and starts viewing it as a signal.

And signals get bought differently.

Not slowly.

Urgently.

Urgency is not always panic.

Sometimes urgency is the recognition that tomorrow might not behave like yesterday.

During most stress events, the system still tries to preserve the appearance of order.

Messaging. Reassurance. Interventions. Sometimes new rules. Sometimes quiet use of the system's tools.

But a silver stress event tends to reveal a truth the system cannot talk its way around.

Scarcity can be delayed.

It cannot be erased.

Eventually the market forces recognition.

And silver, because it sits at the intersection of money and industry, forces recognition faster than many assets.

This is when the canary becomes a spotlight.

Not because it wants chaos.

Because it reveals what the room is built on.

A silver stress event reveals whether trust is abundant or fragile.

It reveals whether paper is convenience or overreach.

It reveals whether claims are backed by substance or backed by assumption.

And once people see that, the game changes.

People can tolerate inflation if they believe it is temporary.

People can tolerate volatility if they believe it is contained.

People can tolerate debt if they believe growth will outpace it.

People can tolerate paper if they believe delivery is always possible.

But when belief in delivery weakens, behavior shifts toward proof.

That migration is what turns a silver stress event from a market moment into a monetary moment.

That is the threshold.

And once it is crossed, silver is not only rising.

Silver is speaking.

Next, we move from what a stress event looks like to why the system fears it.

Because what silver reveals under stress is not only a metal shortage.

It is a confidence shortage.

And confidence shortages are what start new eras.

When confidence breaks, the system discovers what it was really built on.

CHAPTER 12

THE CONFIDENCE SHORTAGE

A **silver shortage is inconvenient.**

A confidence shortage is fatal.

That is the difference.

If you think this book is about metal, you will miss the real story. Silver is not the event. Silver is the instrument. It is the loudest check engine light on the dashboard of a system that runs on faith.

Modern finance does not run on vault doors and gold bars.

It runs on assumptions.

Assumptions that the paper is good.

Assumptions that the counterparty will pay.

Assumptions that the market will be there tomorrow.

Assumptions that liquidity will appear when you need it.

Assumptions that settlement will happen smoothly.

Assumptions that your assets are yours the moment you reach for them.

Assumptions that the rules will not change quickly, quietly, or against you.

The more time you spend inside the system, the more you realize it is not a machine in the mechanical sense.

It is a machine in the psychological sense.

It is built on consensus. Built on compliance. Built on the unspoken agreement that most people will never pull too hard on the fabric.

Because if enough people pull, the system has to reveal what it is made of.

That is what a confidence shortage does.

It pulls.

It tests.

It forces promises to cash out in reality.

And reality is where overpromised systems get exposed.

This is why silver stress events matter to the people who manage the narrative.

Not because a metal getting tight is catastrophic by itself.

Because what it threatens is belief.

The belief that paper is as good as metal.

The belief that markets are deep.

The belief that supply is plentiful.

The belief that settlement is guaranteed.

Once one belief starts cracking, the others start wobbling.

Because confidence is not isolated.

Confidence is a chain.

And chains fail at the weakest link.

Silver is one of those links because it sits at the seam between paper and physical. When silver gets tight, the seam shows. When the seam shows, people begin noticing seams everywhere.

They notice it when a bank limits withdrawals.

They notice it when markets gap open.

They notice it when definitions get revised.

They notice it when "temporary" becomes long-term.

They notice it when the explanation does not match lived experience.

Confidence is rarely lost through argument.

Confidence is lost through mismatch.

And the first time you see that mismatch clearly, it changes you.

You stop assuming.

You start verifying.

You stop trusting narratives.

You start looking for anchors.

That is how a confidence shortage begins.

It does not begin with a statistic.

It begins when ordinary people start making quiet micro-decisions that reveal they no longer believe what they are being told.

They stop saving in cash.

They accelerate purchases.

They keep extra supplies.

They seek stable assets.

They hedge.

They move.

They talk differently.

Most of all, they stop acting like the future is guaranteed.

That behavioral turn is where repricing begins.

Because the system is built on forward behavior.

People buy insurance because they expect tomorrow to arrive.

People buy bonds because they expect repayment.

People hold currency because they expect it to hold meaning.

People buy "safe" assets because they believe safety exists.

Confidence is what turns those beliefs into stable markets.

So when confidence thins, stability thins.

And when stability thins, the system reaches for tools.

Some tools are obvious.

Central bank intervention.

Rate changes.

Liquidity programs.

Emergency statements.

Other tools are quieter.

Reassurance campaigns.

Data revisions.

Regulatory tweaks.

Narrative shaping.

The system always tries to restore confidence because confidence is cheaper than collapse.

But here is the twist.

Sometimes the very tools used to restore confidence also reveal that confidence is failing.

That is the paradox of intervention.

The system steps in to stabilize, and in doing so it tells everyone paying attention that stabilization is needed.

And once people sense stabilization is needed, the next question appears on its own.

Why?

This is how systems get trapped inside their own support.

Every rescue teaches the public that rescues are a feature, not a rare emergency.

Every liquidity program teaches the public that liquidity is engineered.

Every bailout teaches the public that markets are managed.

The system may remain functional.

But the belief shifts.

And belief is the real asset.

So where does silver fit?

Silver is a confidence probe.

Silver is one of the few markets where people can opt out of abstraction in a literal way.

If you distrust a bank, you can withdraw cash, but cash is still the system's currency.

If you distrust a bond, you can sell it, but you are still settling inside the same framework.

If you distrust a stock, you can exit, but you are still inside the financial layer.

Silver is different.

Silver is a form of withdrawal from the premise.

It is the act of saying, I do not want the claim. I want the thing.

When enough people act on that instinct, silver becomes a megaphone for confidence.

Premiums become a mood index.

Availability becomes a trust index.

Delivery becomes a credibility index.

And the most revealing question becomes this.

How hard is the system working to keep silver quiet?

Because the system does not need to manage a market that is not sending a message.

It manages a market when the market is communicating something the system would rather the public not learn too quickly.

Silver communicates that scarcity exists.

Silver communicates that paper claims are not the same as physical supply.

Silver communicates that promises have boundaries.

And boundaries are the one thing paper narratives try to blur.

Because if the public begins thinking in terms of boundaries, it begins thinking in terms of limits.

And once a society thinks in terms of limits, it begins thinking in terms of discipline.

Discipline is the enemy of debt expansion.

Debt expansion is how the modern world has been stabilized for decades.

Debt expansion funds growth.

Debt expansion funds promises.

Debt expansion funds political peace.

Debt expansion funds the illusion that we can have everything now and pay later.

That illusion holds as long as confidence is thick.

But when confidence thins, debt expansion becomes visible.

And once it becomes visible, people start noticing the cost.

Inflation.

Devaluation.

Asset bubbles.

Inequality.

Social tension.

It becomes a different story.

Now make it bigger, because confidence is not only domestic.

It is global.

Reserve currency status is not only economic size.

It is trust at scale.

The world holds dollars because it trusts the dollar system enough to use it.

The world holds U.S. debt because it trusts U.S. collateral enough to treat it as foundational.

But trust is not permanent.

Trust is a relationship.

Relationships change when power shifts, policy gets unpredictable, sanctions become common, politics fractures, debt grows faster than credibility, and alternatives begin forming.

We are in that era.

Which means confidence is being tested from both sides.

Domestically through inflation, debt, and intervention.

Globally through geopolitics, fragmentation, and reserve diversification.

When a system is tested from both sides, it becomes vulnerable to signals.

Signals that make people move.

Signals that make institutions hedge.

Signals that make strategic buyers secure supply.

Silver is one of those signals.

That is why the silver story is not about whether silver rises this year.

It is about whether the world is shifting from confidence-based finance toward proof-based finance.

Confidence-based finance is smooth until it isn't.

Proof-based finance is what people build after they learn trust can be weaponized and promises can be stretched.

Proof-based finance does not mean everyone goes back to coins.

It means people begin valuing assets and systems that reduce counterparty risk.

It means hard collateral matters more.

It means settlement becomes strategic.

It means bridge assets, the ones that live between money and material, become more powerful.

Silver is one of those bridge assets.

So the confidence shortage is not a headline you read.

It is a shift you notice.

People plan differently.

Institutions hedge differently.

Nations build alternatives.

Hard assets get accumulated quietly.

The paper story gets louder and more defensive.

Defensive narratives are always a signal.

They appear when the system is trying to keep the public calm.

Calm keeps the abstraction stable.

Calm keeps people inside the story.

Calm keeps paper functioning like reality.

Silver threatens calm.

Not because it is dramatic.

Because it is physical.

Because it is checkable.

Because it can be owned without asking permission.

That is why silver is feared in a way most people do not understand.

It is not the price.

It is the message.

And once the message spreads, the confidence shortage stops being a quiet leak and becomes a flood.

Next, we move from confidence shortages into the moment confidence becomes policy.

Because when the system senses belief thinning, it does not hope people calm down.

It responds.

And the response reveals the real priorities.

When officials manage belief, you're no longer in a market. You're in a narrative.

CHAPTER 13

WHEN CONFIDENCE BECOMES POLICY

There is a phase in every monetary era when confidence stops being an outcome and becomes a project.

At first, confidence is organic. It rises out of repetition. Paychecks clear. Prices behave. Contracts settle. Institutions feel boring in the best way. People do not think about money because money is doing its job.

Then something shifts.

The system starts needing confidence.

And when a system needs something, it stops waiting for it.

It starts producing it.

That is when confidence becomes policy.

You can feel the pivot before you can prove it.

The language changes first.

Officials stop describing what is happening and start describing what you should believe about what is happening.

The tone goes therapeutic.

The messaging turns rhythmic.

The same phrases reappear like a lullaby played a little too loudly.

Because in a credit-based world, confidence is not a mood.

Confidence is infrastructure.

It is the bridge that keeps promises from being called in.

It is the glue that lets an abstract system function as if it were physical.

It is the cushion between the public and the instinct to demand proof.

When that cushion thins, the system responds the way large systems always respond.

Continuity first.

The first move is almost always narrative, because narrative is cheaper than structural repair.

A story can calm behavior.

A story can buy time.

A story can prevent the two reactions every debt-heavy system fears most.

Runs and flight.

And in the short term, stories work.

They work especially well on people who are busy surviving their own lives.

Most people do not have the time or energy to audit monetary reality. They are raising families, paying bills, managing stress, trying to stay healthy.

Stability is a psychological necessity.

They want something that feels steady enough to build a week on, then a month, then a year.

So the system offers a story you can live inside.

Inflation is temporary.

Deficits are a tool.

Debt is manageable.

The banks are strong.

The markets are orderly.

Liquidity is ample.

Everything is contained.

These are not just phrases.

They are scaffolding.

They hold the mental structure upright long enough for the machine to keep moving.

But people do not live inside phrases.

They live inside groceries, rent, insurance renewals, fuel costs, and paychecks.

They live inside interest rates and credit cards.

They live inside what it feels like to try to get ahead and keep getting pushed back.

When the official story drifts too far from the lived story, the scaffolding starts to creak.

That is when policy stops being mostly guidance and becomes active stabilization.

Words remain.

But now they are paired with visible moves designed to keep behavior from breaking formation.

This is where modern monetary policy becomes less about economics and more about expectation control.

That sounds cynical until you see the mechanics.

In a system built on credit, belief is the load-bearing beam.

So policy protects belief.

Central banks do not only manage inflation.

They manage expectations.

They manage the story people tell themselves about tomorrow.

Because expectations drive behavior.

Behavior drives markets.

Markets drive stability.

Stability is the political floor everything else stands on.

Watch what happens during any real crisis.

The central bank does not only provide liquidity.

It provides a signal.

The adults are here.

Settlement will continue.

The doors will open tomorrow.

That signal is often more important than the liquidity itself.

Because if the signal fails, liquidity is just numbers in a pipe no one trusts.

You can inject cash into a market.

You cannot inject trust into a nervous system that has decided the room is unsafe.

When people stop feeling safe, the system escalates.

This is where confidence-policy becomes tangible.

This is where it starts touching ordinary life.

Rules change.

Quietly at first.

Then openly.

Not always as restrictions. Sometimes as incentives. Sometimes as "temporary measures." Sometimes as safety upgrades.

Different names, same purpose.

Keep behavior inside the lines.

Keep capital inside the system.

Keep the public from turning "exposure" into "delivery."

Keep the fabric from being pulled.

This is the part most people miss.

Management has a side effect.

It teaches.

Repeated interventions teach the public that stability is being produced, not earned.

That markets are being guided toward calm.

That liquidity is engineered.

That support is structural.

And once people learn that, they start asking a new set of questions.

What else is being managed?

What else is held together by scaffolding?

Where else does the official picture rely on cooperation?

This is where we return to silver, and we do it without repeating the prior point.

Silver is not just a hedge.

Silver is a stress test you can perform personally.

You cannot hold GDP.

You cannot withdraw CPI.

You cannot touch policy credibility.

But you can try to buy silver.

You can watch premiums.

You can watch availability.

You can watch delivery timelines.

You can watch the gap between the paper number and the physical experience widen or close in real time.

That makes silver a reality check in an era where confidence is increasingly curated.

A managed-confidence system needs symbols to function like substance.

It needs paper to behave like metal.

It needs people to remain satisfied with claims.

But when physical availability contradicts the symbol, the story stops feeling smooth.

And when the story stops feeling smooth, it does not stay confined to one market.

It changes the mental model people use for everything else.

Here is the key insight of this section.

When confidence becomes policy, stability changes meaning.

Stability stops being something the system earns through strength.

Stability becomes something the system maintains through tools.

And maintained stability can look flawless right up until the moment it fails.

Because enforcement is not resilience.

Enforcement is pressure.

Pressure accumulates.

That is why the most dangerous periods are rarely the loud ones.

They are the calm-looking ones where the system is working hardest behind the scenes to keep the surface still.

That is when fragility grows quietly.

That is when small signals matter.

That is when the canary matters.

Because the canary does not care about reassurance.

The canary reacts to air.

Silver reacts to reality.

And reality has a way of cutting through even the most polished confidence project.

Next, we step into what this evolves into in practice.

Not science fiction.

Feedback loops.

Digital rails that make policy faster, more targeted, more enforceable.

When confidence becomes policy, the next step is building infrastructure that can manage behavior with less delay.

That is where the future stops sounding futuristic.

And that is where silver becomes more relevant, because the hunger for proof does not disappear in a more digital world.

It concentrates.

CHAPTER 14

THE SILVER WAR

Wars do not always look like wars.

Some are fought with missiles and maps. Some are fought with tariffs and treaties. Some are fought with sanctions, subpoenas, and late-night calls between people whose names never land in a headline.

And some wars are fought inside markets.

Not with soldiers.

With supply.

With contracts.

With leverage.

With settlement rules.

With the quiet power of deciding who gets delivery and who gets offered cash and a smile.

That is the silver war.

You can miss it completely if you only watch the price.

Because the silver war is not just about where silver trades.

It is about who controls the story of silver.

Who controls the flow of silver.

Who has the right to claim silver.

Who gets physical.

Who gets paper.

And who gets crushed between the two.

The reason this is contested is simple.

Silver is both money and material.

It carries thousands of years of monetary memory, and it sits inside the hardware of the future.

Anything that lives at the intersection of money and necessity becomes strategic.

Anything strategic becomes fought over.

Anything fought over becomes a battlefield.

So stop thinking of silver as a sleepy commodity.

Think of it as contested ground.

Contested ground does not move cleanly.

It moves in feints and reversals.

It moves in false breakouts and sudden slams.

It moves in squeezes and flushes.

It moves in ways that discourage conviction.

And that discouragement is not random.

In contested markets, confusion is a weapon.

The objective is not only to win.

The objective is to exhaust.

To disorient.

To make the asset feel unreliable so fewer people hold it with patience and certainty.

That matters because silver is a message asset whether the system admits it or not.

A sharp, sustained rise in silver broadcasts things the system would rather keep quiet.

It suggests currency confidence is thinning.

It suggests inflation is closer to the surface than the rhetoric.

It suggests paper promises have edges.

It suggests the public is migrating toward hard collateral.

That message is destabilizing, because belief is load-bearing in a credit world.

So the silver war is, in part, a war against that message.

This does not require a cartoon villain.

It only requires incentives.

There are powerful incentives for silver to remain calm, heavy, and frustrating.

Quiet metals imply quiet fear.

Quiet metals imply trust.

Quiet metals imply the currency story is intact.

Silver is dangerous because it is sensitive enough to reflect stress quickly and affordable enough for ordinary people to touch it.

It can turn a macro problem into a physical experience.

The conflict shows up on three fronts.

Paper.

Physical.

Psychological.

The paper front is where the visible action lives.

Futures, options, derivatives, and synthetic products dominate volume.

That means the reference price is often set by paper flow rather than metal changing hands.

In a structure like that, price can be shoved around without a single bar leaving a vault.

Contracts can be sold, claims can be created, and rallies can be made to feel like they are lifting a weight.

You can feel it in the rhythm.

The breakout that gets swatted.

The rally that gets capped.

The drop that arrives on a surge of paper while physical demand stays stubborn.

That is the paper front.

The physical front is quieter, and it is where the war becomes real.

Physical buyers do not care about tricks.

They care about metal.

And when physical demand rises, the system meets constraints it cannot argue with.

Inventories draw down.

Delivery schedules stretch.

Premiums rise.

Mints ration.

Fabricators backlog.

Industrial buyers lock contracts.

Strategic buyers accumulate.

Paper can multiply claims.

It cannot multiply bars.

Every contested system has a moment where abstraction touches reality.

In silver, that moment is delivery.

The psychological front is the one most people underestimate, and it is where most people lose.

Because the silver war is also fought inside the mind.

It is fought in patience.

It is fought in fatigue.

It is fought in the slow drip of disappointment that makes people abandon the position right before the structure is forced to reprice.

Silver is unusually good at testing endurance.

It can climb slowly and get slammed.

It can build hope and punish it.

It can make you feel early, then late, then foolish.

In contested markets, that churn is not a side effect.

It is a strategy.

The best way to prevent a rush is to prevent conviction.

If the public stays uncertain, it does not pile in.

If the public stays tired, it does not hold.

If the public stays distracted, it does not notice the physical constraints forming underneath the paper stage.

Time becomes a weapon.

So does distraction.

Keep the crowd chasing louder narratives, and fewer people listen to the canary.

Meanwhile, the physical market tightens quietly.

This is how serious players accumulate.

They do not buy when the crowd is screaming.

They buy when the crowd is bored.

Here is the part that makes this story worth reading.

The war is not one-sided.

Silver has physics on its side.

Silver has necessity.

Silver has constraint.

Those forces can be delayed, managed, and masked.

They cannot be erased.

Eventually pressure crosses a threshold.

Physical demand bites hard enough that the paper front has to adapt.

That adaptation can look like a squeeze, a gap, a sudden repricing, a move so violent it feels like an ambush to anyone who decided silver was dead.

Silver explosions feel like ambushes because they are the moment the war becomes visible.

The physical front breaks through the paper front.

Psychology flips from exhaustion to urgency.

And once urgency appears, the structure gets unstable for one reason.

Paper systems are held together by behavior.

Rolling contracts.

Accepting cash settlement.

Trusting that delivery is always possible even if you never ask for it.

When behavior shifts away from cooperation, the system feels pain.

Silver is one of the few assets where people can opt out in a literal way.

They can remove metal from the board.

And when enough metal gets removed, paper starts competing with reality.

That competition is where the silver war reaches its climax.

This is not just a story about banks and nations.

It is fought inside ordinary people.

People who do not want to gamble.

They want to protect.

People who do not want obsession.

They want preparation.

People who do not want to beat the system.

They want a way to store value that does not depend on the same abstraction that keeps making them uneasy.

When enough people share that instinct, the silver war changes shape.

Because the line is simple.

Does the public remain compliant with claims.

Or does it migrate toward proof.

That is the real contest.

And it is getting closer.

You can feel it in the cost of living.

In the disconnect between official tone and lived math.

In thinning trust.

In nations building alternatives.

In new rails being laid.

All of it points to one plain conclusion.

We are moving into an era where proof becomes premium.

Silver is proof.

So the silver war is not a niche story.

It is one front in the larger fight over what money will be, what collateral will matter, who controls settlement, and who is left holding promises when the world begins prioritizing substance.

Next, we take on the most dangerous myth in modern finance.
The idea that the system can always print its way out.
Printing can fix liquidity.
It cannot repair belief.
And silver sits exactly where those two realities collide.
Liquidity buys time. Trust decides the future.

CHAPTER 15

YOU CAN PRINT LIQUIDITY, YOU CAN'T PRINT TRUST

I have heard people say it like it is a superpower.

They will just print.

It comes with that half-smirk, half-shrug delivery. Like the game is rigged, but also simple. Like the system has a cheat code. Like anyone expecting consequences has not read the manual.

On one level, that instinct is correct.

In a fiat system, authorities can manufacture liquidity. They can expand the balance sheet, backstop banks, buy assets, and turn a panic into a policy event. They can make fear feel temporary. They can keep the gears turning long after the metal is tired.

That is the design.

But the phrase "they will just print" collapses two very different problems into one.

Printing can solve a liquidity shortage.

Printing cannot solve a trust shortage.

And when printing becomes obvious, it can accelerate the trust shortage, because printing is not only a tool.

It is a signal.

It signals that the system could not clear on its own.

It signals that the promises required reinforcement.

It signals that normalcy is being maintained, not naturally produced.

Once people sense that, questions appear that do not go back in the box.

How much support is temporary and how much is now permanent.

How much of the economy is organic and how much is scaffolding.

How much of the value in my money is earned and how much is maintained.

Those questions do not live only in spreadsheets.

They live in the nervous system.

Money is not just purchasing power.

Money is planning.

Money is predictability.

Money is the quiet confidence that tomorrow will rhyme with yesterday well enough for you to make decisions today.

So when people begin to feel the system is being maintained rather than functioning, behavior shifts.

They stop assuming.

They start hedging.

They hold less idle currency.

They move toward assets that feel less dependent on continual rescue.

That is where this stops being academic and becomes mechanical.

If a bank is wobbling, liquidity can keep depositors whole and prevent a freeze.

If a bond market is disorderly, a central bank can step in as a buyer to calm it.

If markets are spiraling, rates can be cut, programs can be launched, statements can be issued, and the system can be guided back toward the appearance of stability.

Liquidity is grease.

Central banks have become the world's industrial suppliers of it.

But grease is not strength.

Grease reduces visible friction.

It does not repair stressed structure.

So when someone says "they will just print," what they are really saying is "they will just grease."

And greasing works until it changes the one thing the entire structure depends on.

Currency credibility.

Every visible intervention teaches a subtle lesson.

The money supply is elastic.

The rules are adjustable.

The promise is managed.

In calm seasons, people file that away as policy.

In stressed seasons, the same lesson lands differently.

It lands as doubt.

Because under stress, people do not only want liquidity.

They want certainty.

They want an anchor.

They want something that does not require repeated stabilization to keep its meaning.

Liquidity is functional.

Trust is existential.

A cleaner metaphor than printing is this.

Liquidity is the water.

Trust is the riverbed.

You can pour more water into a river.

But if the riverbed fractures, water stops looking like flow and starts looking like flood.

It changes course.

It eats the banks.

It destroys the structures built around it.

That fracture point is why late-stage fiat cycles feel strange.

The same actions that once calmed the crowd start producing diminishing returns.

The first rescue reassures.

The fifth rescue raises eyebrows.

The tenth rescue changes belief.

Rate cuts that used to feel like relief begin to feel like dependency.

Emergency programs that used to feel protective begin to feel like confession.

Not because the tool changed.

Because the audience changed.

Trust decays when people sense that increasingly extreme measures are required to preserve the appearance of normal.

This is how printing becomes a trap.

Once the public expects printing, they begin expecting dilution.

Once they expect dilution, they begin spending and positioning faster.

Once behavior speeds up, inflation psychology hardens.

Once inflation psychology hardens, policymakers tighten.

Tightening breaks something.

Then printing returns.

That loop is how a currency starts feeling less like a stable tool and more like a moving target.

This is why you can print liquidity, but you cannot print trust.

Trust has to be earned.

And once it is bruised, it becomes expensive to repair.

Now the silver connection sharpens.

When trust thins, people search for assets that sit outside the policy loop. They want value that does not require continuous reinforcement to remain believable.

Gold is the traditional move.

Silver is the accessible move.

But silver has a special role in this phase because it is not only owned.

It is held.

It provides a physical yes in a world of digital maybes.

Not as ideology.

As relief.

Most people do not need monetary theory to understand weight.

They understand the difference between a number and a thing.

That difference becomes emotionally powerful when the world starts feeling like promises stacked on promises.

And there is a second edge to silver that makes "they will just print" collide with reality.

Printing can produce liquidity.

Printing cannot produce metal.

It cannot create mine supply overnight.

It cannot expand refinery capacity on demand.

It cannot fix delivery constraints in the short term.

So the more the system relies on printing to calm stress, the more it can motivate the search for proof, and the more that search can pressure physical supply.

That is the irony.

The same action used to stabilize the abstraction can intensify the desire to exit the abstraction.

That is when silver becomes combustible.

It is small enough to be stressed.

Necessary enough to matter.

Recognizable enough to spread.

Easy enough for ordinary people to remove from the paper ecosystem.

And tied enough to industry that it is not purely a sentiment trade.

So the real question is not can they print.

They can.

The question is whether they can maintain belief while they print.

Because if belief does not hold, printing stops being water and starts being gasoline.

It accelerates the migration into hard collateral.

It accelerates the repricing of scarcity.

It accelerates the silver war.

And once printing loses its calming effect, the next reflex shows up.

Tighter control mechanisms.

Not always to punish.

To preserve continuity.

To keep behavior inside the abstraction.

To make trust less necessary by making movement more governable.

That is where digital money stops being a tech story and starts becoming a governance story.

The more programmable money becomes, the more conditional freedom becomes.

CHAPTER 16
PROGRAMMABLE MONEY, CONDITIONAL FREEDOM

The first time I heard someone say "programmable money" out loud, it was framed like a victory lap.

Sleeker rails. Faster settlement. Fewer middlemen. Cleaner compliance. Better fraud controls. More safety.

If you only stare at the surface, it reads like progress.

Then I did the one thing you do when a pitch sounds too polished.

I asked the question the pitch avoids.

Programmable for who?

Because money is never only money.

Money is permission.

Mobility.

Options.

The ability to say no.

The ability to leave.

The ability to build.

The ability to survive without asking for approval.

So when someone says "programmable money," what they are

really describing is a system where permission, mobility, options, and survival can be governed by code.

And code does not care about your intentions.

Code cares about rules.

That is the hinge.

A programmable currency can be a tool for efficiency.

It can also become a tool for control.

Not in a cinematic dystopia on day one.

In the most believable way possible.

The "we need stability" way.

The "we need to prevent fraud" way.

The "we need to enforce compliance" way.

The "we need to keep the system from breaking" way.

This is where the prior chapter matters without being repeated.

When a system enters a trust-thin era, it stops relying on persuasion alone and starts building mechanisms that shape behavior at the source.

Not because every actor is malicious.

Because large systems under stress prefer predictable outcomes.

Programmable money is the ultimate predictability tool.

It does not only influence behavior.

It can limit behavior.

It can be targeted.

It can be throttled.

It can be restricted by category, geography, time window, risk score, or policy condition.

It can be frozen.

It can be made to expire.

It can be switched off.

That is why the phrase feels harmless until you translate it into plain English.

Programmable money means conditional money.

And conditional money means someone else can decide what your money is allowed to do.

This is where people get trapped arguing extremes, so keep it grounded.

The risk is not that every digital currency becomes tyranny.

The risk is that the capability exists.

And in periods of stress, capabilities migrate toward use.

History does not need villains to produce controls.

It only needs fear.

When societies feel threatened, they accept measures they would have rejected when they felt safe.

They trade autonomy for stability because they are human, because they have families, because they want the noise to stop.

So if we are moving into an era defined by debt pressure, persistent inflation psychology, geopolitical fragmentation, and trust fatigue, the incentive to build manageability tools is obvious.

A programmable currency makes the system easier to manage.

Stimulus can be aimed with precision.

Sanctions can be enforced with less leakage.

Taxes can be collected with fewer loopholes.

Policy can execute instantly.

Friction drops.

Visibility rises.

And exit routes narrow.

That last part never makes the brochure.

But it is always present in the architecture.

Because any system that depends on broad participation cannot treat mass exits as neutral.

In calm times, exits feel like freedom.

In stressed times, exits feel like threat.

This is why capital controls appear in monetary stress cycles.

Not as theatrics.

As triage.

Programmable money is capital control with a user interface.

It can arrive quietly.

It can be branded as modernization.

Most people will not notice the cage being assembled because the bars look like features.

And that leads to the central tension of this chapter.

The more programmable money becomes, the more people seek less programmable value.

That is not ideology.

It is reflex.

When conditions begin attaching themselves to your options, you start valuing options like oxygen.

This is where silver becomes more relevant, not less.

Silver is the opposite of conditional money.

It cannot be updated by a policy patch.

It cannot be frozen with a keystroke.

It cannot be made to expire.

It cannot be permissioned by category or location.

It exists outside the logic of code.

And in a world where the monetary layer becomes more software-like, assets outside the software layer gain psychological gravity.

People do not need to become rebels to want a back door.

They only need to be honest about what tools do in the wrong hands or in the wrong season.

Now widen the lens.

This does not stop at individuals.

Programmable money reshapes geopolitics.

If settlement becomes code-enforced, the party that controls the code gains leverage.

Leverage over access.

Leverage over trade.

Leverage over liquidity.

Leverage over who gets to move value and who gets slowed, filtered, or stopped.

That is why nations build alternate rails.

That is why they diversify reserves.

That is why they secure strategic inputs.

Because the next conflicts will often look like access, not armies.

Access to settlement.

Access to markets.

Access to supply.

Access to liquidity.

In a programmable world, access becomes power.

And here is the deeper game most people miss.

Rails are not enough without resources.

You can control the plumbing and still lose the water.

You can dominate settlement and still be vulnerable to material constraint.

So the future becomes a contest between code and atoms.

Between control systems and constrained materials.

Between the ability to enforce rules and the reality that certain inputs cannot be conjured by decree.

Silver sits in the overlap.

It is an opt-out asset for citizens.

It is a required input for infrastructure.

Exit and necessity in the same material.

And when an asset plays both roles, it does not remain quiet forever.

It becomes a pressure point.

Not because it is dramatic.

Because it is unavoidable.

So the real question is not whether programmable money can be built.

It is being built.

The question is what happens when a programmable monetary layer tightens at the same time the physical layer tightens.

Because when both layers tighten, the system becomes more sensitive to shocks.

Cutoffs hurt more.

Shortages bite harder.

And the demand for proof rises, not as a trend, but as a survival instinct dressed in everyday clothing.

That is why physical silver stays psychologically potent.

It is simple.

It is real.

It is yours when you hold it.

In a world where ownership increasingly means authorized access, that kind of ownership starts feeling like sovereignty.

Not political sovereignty.

Personal sovereignty.

A small, silent counterweight.

So keep the frame clear as we move forward.

If rails become more programmable and the world becomes more resource-constrained, the collision is not a metaphor.

It is a behavioral event.

And once behavior turns toward proof at scale, silver does not need marketing.

Silver becomes unavoidable.

CHAPTER 17

THE RUSH TOWARD PROOF

There is a particular kind of silence right before a crowd moves.

If you have ever been in an airport when a storm hits, you know it.

The announcements start. Delays stack. People check their phones more often. Conversations shorten.

Everyone keeps pretending they are calm, but the room changes temperature.

The air turns alert.

People start guarding their options.

Then a gate agent says one sentence like, "We have limited seats on the next available flight."

And the performance ends.

People stand. Lines form. Voices rise.

Not because humans become animals.

Because scarcity stops being abstract.

It becomes physical.

It becomes now.

That is what a rush toward proof looks like.

And when it happens in money, it rarely begins with ideology.

It begins with friction.

A hold that was never there before.

A transfer that takes longer than it should.

A transaction that gets denied without explanation.

A new rule that appears without consent.

Essentials that jump in price and stay there.

A "safe" asset that starts acting unfamiliar.

None of those moments is catastrophic on its own.

But they teach.

They teach the public that the system has gates.

And once people notice gates, they ask the only question that matters.

Who controls them?

That question is the seed.

Proof is what people reach for when gatekeeping becomes visible.

Proof is what you want when access feels conditional.

Proof is what you want when rules feel flexible.

Proof is what you want when ownership starts sounding like authorized access.

This is why late-cycle behavior is so consistent across history.

When trust thins, people move toward tangible things.

Things that can be held.

Things that do not require permission.

Sometimes land.

Sometimes inventory.

Sometimes tools.

Sometimes gold.

Often silver, because it sits at the reachable end of the proof spectrum.

And the most important shift happens quietly.

The rush toward proof begins slowly.

Then it accelerates.

Because proof is contagious.

Not in a social-media way.

In a human way.

When one person acts like the system might behave differently under stress, other people do not need a lecture.

They recognize the signal.

Behavior spreads.

In finance, behavior spread is what turns concern into a run.

That is why the system fears a rush toward proof more than it fears any single statistic.

It can manage numbers for a while.

It can massage headlines for a while.

It can add liquidity for a while.

But once behavior crosses a threshold, management gets expensive.

Now put silver in this frame.

Silver is proof that still feels accessible.

Gold is proof too, but gold carries a psychological distance for many people.

Silver feels like something an ordinary person can reach for without joining a different social class.

That matters because silver is not built to absorb a stampede.

The retail pipeline is tuned for steady demand, not mass urgency.

So when the rush starts, constraints show up fast.

Dealers run thin.

Mints fall behind.

Premiums jump.

Backorders normalize.

Availability becomes the headline.

And once availability becomes the headline, the rush feeds itself.

Because nobody wants to discover the exit when the hallway is already packed.

Retail is the spark.

The wildfire begins when institutions tilt the same direction.

Institutions do not need fear to move.

They need risk.

They see the plumbing.

They understand collateral.

They understand that when public behavior shifts, liquidity can vanish.

They understand that the best time to reach the exit is before the crowd makes it obvious.

So institutional movement toward proof looks calm on the outside.

It shows up as small reallocations, quiet procurement, custody preference, higher collateral standards, a subtle refusal to rely on promises when reality is available.

And when large money leans toward physical, silver tightens fast.

The market is simply not that deep.

This is where the rush collides with the paper machine.

Paper can expand claims.

Paper can keep a price orderly for a while.

Paper can offer exposure at scale.

Paper cannot renegotiate one fact.

Physical is finite.

Finite things behave differently when demand turns urgent.

That is the moment the split starts widening.

The paper number stays calm, while the physical world gets loud.

Premiums become a language.

Delivery becomes the issue.

Cash settlement becomes a pressure-release valve.

And the system starts doing what systems do when a crowd stands up.

It tries to slow the crowd down.

Here is the deeper point, and it is the one that keeps this section from repeating earlier chapters.

A rush toward proof is not a single event.

It is a learning curve.

Once people feel the difference between ownership and access, they do not unlearn it.

Once they watch the system behave differently under stress, they do not forget it.

The next shock does not need to convince them.

It only needs to remind them.

So the rush arrives in waves.

A series of lessons.

Each wave trains the next one to move earlier.

And in a world where narratives can mutate fast, those waves can be triggered faster than physical supply chains can respond.

That mismatch is why proof rushes can feel sudden.

And why silver, because it is both accessible and physical, often becomes one of the first doors the public tries to push open.

When that door starts sticking, power answers.

Not with a speech.

With rules.

And the rules tell you what the future values most.

CHAPTER 18

WHEN POWER ANSWERS

You can learn more about a system in the five minutes it feels threatened than in ten years of normal life.

When a system feels secure, it can afford virtue.

It can afford patience.

It can afford to look principled.

It can tolerate debate, inefficiency, even a little chaos, because the foundation feels solid.

When a system feels threatened, it stops performing.

It reveals what it protects.

It reveals what it fears.

It reveals how far it will go to preserve continuity.

And in money, power rarely answers with speeches first.

It answers with mechanics.

Rules.

Incentives.

Gates.

Friction placed precisely where people try to leave.

Because in a trust-based system, the public has one power that terrifies every central authority.

The power to withdraw belief.

The power to withdraw participation.

The power to stop playing along.

A rush toward proof is simply that power becoming visible.

It is the public saying, even quietly, I want less dependence on your story.

Modern systems do not need to crush that instinct with force.

They only need to make it inconvenient enough that most people decide it is not worth it.

That is how control works now.

Not boots in the street.

Friction in the pipes.

Here is the frame that matters for this chapter.

Earlier, we described what a rush toward proof looks like.

Now we are describing what the system does next.

It tends to move in stages.

Not because there is a conspiracy meeting.

Because large institutions respond to stress the same way large organisms do.

Stabilize first.

Then steer.

Then harden.

Stage one is reassurance.

The messaging turns repetitive, therapeutic, confident by volume.

Everything is fine.

Markets are stable.

Banks are strong.

Inflation is contained.

The point is not information.

The point is nervous system management.

Reassurance works because it has a customer base.

People want normal life.

They want tomorrow to look like yesterday.

But reassurance has a weakness.

Reality.

If lived experience keeps contradicting the story, the story stops calming.

It starts irritating.

It becomes noise.

That is when stage two begins.

Intervention.

Not words.

Action.

Backstops.

Emergency facilities.

Liquidity injections.

Rule changes framed as temporary.

The machine is kept running, and for a time it works, because liquidity can solve immediate plumbing problems.

But intervention teaches a lesson all by itself.

It tells the public what would have happened without it.

It reveals fragility.

And once fragility is visible, a portion of the public still moves toward proof.

Only now they move with more conviction.

Because the system has confirmed the thing it hoped to hide.

The normal state requires support.

That is when stage three begins.

Behavioral steering.

This is the part most people feel but cannot name.

The system stops trying to convince you and starts trying to guide you.

Not by banning exits outright.

By redesigning the incentive map.

Yield here.

Restrictions there.

Tax preferences.

Reporting thresholds.

Compliance updates.

New categories of safety.

Conveniences that make participation frictionless.

Friction that makes opting out feel like stepping into a storm.

The point is not confrontation.

The point is flow.

Money is treated like water.

You do not need to stop water to control it.

You shape the channel.

You decide where it moves easily and where it meets resistance.

This is the modern answer.

And this is where silver becomes uniquely relevant, because silver is one of the few forms of proof that cannot be patched out of existence.

You can make it inconvenient.

You can make it annoying.

You can attack it through paper flows and narrative.

You can try to keep it quiet.

But you cannot update the software and remove atoms from the Earth.

You cannot freeze a bar sitting in someone's safe.

You cannot turn off what is already outside the rails.

Now zoom out one more level.

In a more programmable monetary world, the system gains something prior eras never had at scale.

Real-time leverage over behavior.

Transactions can be restricted by category, by geography, by time, by risk scoring.

Flows can be seen instantly.

Incentives can be adjusted quickly.

That is efficiency.

It is also soft control.

Soft control turns into hard control under stress, because stress changes what people accept.

When people feel threatened, they trade autonomy for perceived safety.

Not because they are weak.

Because they are human.

That is the paradox you need the reader to feel in their gut.

The moves used to preserve stability can erode the trust that makes stability cheap.

The system intervenes to calm markets.

The intervention signals fragility.

The system tightens rules to maintain order.

The tightening signals fear.

The system rewards participation to keep rails full.

The rewards signal dependency.

And once people sense dependency, demand for proof grows.

This is the conflict line stated cleanly.

The system wants behavior inside the rails.

The public wants options outside the rails.

That is the real war.

Not good versus evil.

Continuity versus autonomy.

Managed trust versus demanded proof.

Now the final turn that sets up the next chapter without repeating anything.

Power does not rely on control alone.

Control creates backlash.

So the more effective strategy is a new deal.

Convenience so seductive that opting out feels like choosing hardship.

That is how the cage becomes comfortable.

That is how it becomes popular.

That is how people trade autonomy for ease without feeling coerced.

And that is why silver does not become irrelevant in this era.

It becomes the quiet insurance policy for the minority who want an option that does not require permission.

Next, we move into the human layer.

What people actually do when they sense this shift, not as politics, but as planning.

The small decisions that add up.

The quiet forms of resistance that look less like protest and more like preparation.

CHAPTER 19
QUIET RESISTANCE

Most people hear the word resistance and picture a protest.

Signs.

Megaphones.

Crowds in the street.

A dramatic showdown where somebody wins and somebody loses.

Financial eras rarely turn that way.

Monetary resistance is quieter.

It is domestic.

It is private.

It looks less like defiance and more like design.

A family that stops trusting the default settings.

A person who used to keep everything in one place deciding they want options.

A business owner diversifying suppliers because a single point of failure suddenly feels reckless.

A saver moving part of their value into things that do not depend on a password, a platform, or a policy update.

This is the mirror chapter.

We already covered the system's answer.

Reassurance.

Intervention.

Steering.

Now we cover the public's answer back.

Without speeches.

Without politics.

Without needing permission.

Most people do not want conflict.

They want continuity.

But they also want dignity.

They want autonomy.

They want the ability to protect their families without having to audition for access in a system that can change the rules quietly.

So resistance, in the monetary sense, is not always rebellion.

It is adaptability.

It is redundancy.

It is distributed resilience.

It is people restoring contact with reality after living too long inside abstractions.

That shift shows up as small behaviors that look boring until you notice what they signal.

Paying down high-interest debt faster.

Keeping emergency reserves.

Diversifying where money sits and how it is stored.

Learning skills that make life less fragile.

Building buffers that do not require perfect conditions to work.

They do not call it resistance.

They call it common sense.

But common sense becomes resistance inside a system that depends on compliance with the default.

Because the default is the business model.

Now bring silver back into focus, but keep it clean.

Silver is not a slogan.

It is not anti-technology.

It is not a personality.

Silver is redundancy that fits in ordinary hands.

It is pro-option.

In the world we are moving into, options become more valuable than convenience, because convenience becomes conditional.

Conditionality is the moment people wake up.

Not when a commentator warns them.

When their own access changes.

This is where systems misjudge the public.

They assume resistance will be loud.

It rarely is.

When pressure rises, people stop talking publicly and start acting privately.

They do not need a movement.

They need a backup.

That is why metals gain force under stress.

They are private resilience.

Quiet insurance.

Options you do not have to announce to use.

If you own silver, you do not need a platform to keep it real.

You do not need a policy update to keep it valid.

You do not need permission for it to exist.

That is the clean reason it keeps returning across eras.

Silver survives because it solves a simple human problem.

How to keep choices alive when conditions change.

Now make it practical.

Resistance shows up in three lanes.

First, households.

Slow accumulation.

Steady removal of physical supply from circulation.

Not dramatic.

Persistent.

The kind of pressure that does not trend until it matters.

Second, institutions.

Quiet repositioning toward custody, collateral quality, and assets that reduce counterparty risk.

Not because they are scared.

Because they are paid to see plumbing.

Third, strategic procurement.

Industries and nations securing inputs, locking supply, building redundancy.

This demand is sticky.

It does not disappear when the news cycle changes.

When those three lanes lean the same direction at once, silver stops behaving like a sleepy commodity and starts behaving like a pressure gauge.

Not because anybody declared war.

Because behavior changed.

And behavior is what breaks models.

One layer makes this era different, and it is not ideology.

It is speed.

Resistance is now networked.

In prior eras, people made these shifts in isolation.

Now proof spreads socially.

Premium spikes travel faster than supply chains can react.

A shortage becomes a viral story.

A clip becomes urgency.

A rumor becomes a run.

Silver cannot scale at internet speed.

Mines do not respond to trending topics.

Refineries do not expand because a hashtag went up.

That mismatch is why volatility rises in this phase.

The behavior layer accelerates.

The physical layer stays stubborn.

Now the point that earns the chapter title.

Resistance is not the enemy of stability.

It is the immune response that prevents systems from becoming so brittle they shatter.

If nobody ever built redundancy, fragility would accumulate quietly until failure arrived as a surprise.

Resistance forces alternatives.

It forces buffers.

It forces systems to face their own weak points.

Silver is one expression of that immune response.

Not the only one.

One of the most accessible.

One of the most checkable.

One of the most human.

So this chapter is not telling people to fight.

It is showing them how eras actually shift.

Not through one dramatic event.

Through a thousand small decisions that quietly change what the world demands.

Next, we go one level higher.

What happens when this quiet resistance becomes normal behavior.

When proof stops being niche and starts being culture.

Because when proof becomes the trend, the abstraction stops feeling inevitable.

And that is when the old system starts losing its grip.

First on narrative.

Then on the next generation's instincts.

CHAPTER 20

WHEN PROOF BECOMES CULTURAL

For most of modern life, trust has been outsourced.

You trust the bank because it is regulated.

You trust the grocery store because the supply chain keeps showing up.

You trust the currency because everyone else does.

You trust the news because it looks official.

You trust the system because you have never been forced to pressure-test it.

That is what a stable era feels like.

You do not spend your days verifying basic reality.

You live.

You plan.

You build.

You assume.

Then the contradictions start stacking.

Not one headline.

Not one crisis.

A pattern.

Small mismatches that keep repeating until your nervous system notices before your brain can explain why.

The official story stays smooth while lived experience gets rougher.

Prices climb, then normalize on paper while your receipts refuse to cooperate.

Rules shift quietly.

Services degrade.

Exceptions become standard.

And the public begins doing the one thing that changes everything.

They stop assuming.

They start verifying.

At first it looks fringe.

A few people ask annoying questions.

A few people buy hard assets.

A few people use phrases like sound money.

A few people get laughed at and dismissed as paranoid, political, extreme, old-fashioned, or obsessed.

That is usually where the story stays until life forces the issue.

Because culture does not change through debate.

Culture changes through experience.

When enough people experience the same instability at the same time, behavior shifts become mainstream.

That is the moment proof becomes cultural.

And when proof becomes cultural, a system built on abstraction starts feeling exposed.

Abstraction works when most people are calm.

Abstraction fails when most people demand verification.

This is why the rush toward proof is not the real tipping point.

The real tipping point is when the rush becomes normal.

When the impulse to verify becomes mainstream behavior.

When hard assets stop feeling like a quirky hobby and start feeling like basic responsibility.

When holding physical value becomes socially acceptable.

When people stop asking why would you do that.

And start asking how do I do that.

That is when proof becomes cultural.

And once it becomes cultural, it does not reverse easily.

It becomes identity.

It becomes habit.

It becomes what responsible people do.

That is the difference between a temporary panic and an era shift.

Temporary panic fades.

Cultural shifts persist.

We have already watched early versions of this in other parts of life.

People keep extra supplies now.

People stockpile certain essentials now.

People talk about self-reliance, redundancy, and alternatives in health, education, work, even community.

The trend is not random.

It is a response to trust thinning.

It is the culture pivoting from centralized trust to distributed resilience.

Money is the final frontier of that pivot.

Because money is where dependency has been deepest and most invisible.

Money has been the last thing most people questioned because it is the backbone of daily life.

So when proof becomes cultural in money, it is bigger than finance.

It is a social evolution.

The driver is not ideology.

It is lived experience.

Inflation that does not fully unwind.

Rent rising faster than wages.

Debt that feels permanent.

Institutions losing credibility.

Narratives getting louder while reality gets harder.

A future that feels managed instead of stable.

And once enough people feel that, proof begins to feel like dignity.

This is why people who buy silver often sound different than people who buy stocks.

Stock buyers talk like opportunity.

Silver buyers talk like protection.

One is about winning.

One is about not losing what matters.

When proof becomes cultural, that protective instinct goes mainstream.

Because mainstream life begins feeling like it has something to lose that it cannot risk losing.

Stability.

Autonomy.

Predictability.

A future that makes sense.

Silver matters in this cultural shift for one simple reason.

It is socially portable.

Gold has always carried a wealth aura.

It feels like something you buy after you are stable.

Silver feels like something you buy while you are trying to become stable.

It is the first proof asset most normal people can reach for without a fortune.

It is the metal you can hand to a teenager and say, this is real.

It is weight you can understand without a finance degree.

Silver is a bridge between abstraction and substance.

And bridges are how movements spread.

Now here is the part most people do not see coming.

When proof becomes cultural, demand structure changes permanently.

It is not just panic buying during a scary week.

It becomes recurring accumulation.

It becomes lifestyle.

It becomes habit.

People start buying silver the way people used to buy savings bonds.

A little each month.

A stack over time.

A routine that turns into resilience.

That habit matters more than any single event, because habits are stable demand.

And stable demand slowly drains supply.

Silver supply is already constrained.

That means cultural adoption can reshape the market without needing a dramatic catalyst.

You do not need a collapse.

You need millions of people making a small decision repeatedly.

That is how eras flip quietly.

And it is why the silver war intensifies as proof becomes cultural.

The system can manage a fringe.

It struggles to manage a habit.

It can dismiss a movement.

It struggles to dismiss a mainstream practice.

It can suppress a narrative.

It struggles to suppress behavior once the behavior becomes normal.

Once proof becomes cultural, the paper market becomes more fragile because the baseline preference shifts toward physical ownership.

That changes everything.

Premiums become more sensitive.

Inventory tightens.

Delivery matters more.

Paper claims get questioned more often.

The gap between paper and physical becomes more visible.

And visible gaps spread faster than any argument, because contradictions you can touch are undefeated.

Now culture and power collide.

When proof becomes cultural, power responds.

Not with panic.

With adaptation.

It tries to absorb the shift.

It offers new products, new instruments, new incentives, new rails.

It offers approved proof.

This is one of the cleverest moves systems make.

They do not always fight proof.

They package it.

Exposure.

Custodial products.

Tokenized versions.

Regulated wrappers designed to satisfy the craving for proof while keeping the public inside the managed lanes.

The system does not fear people owning silver exposure.

The system fears people owning silver.

The difference is custody.

Custody is the battleground.

Custody decides control.

Custody decides access under stress.

Custody decides whether ownership is property or permission.

So when proof becomes cultural, the system will offer substitutes that look like proof while keeping the public at arm's length from the thing itself.

Not necessarily malicious.

Structural.

That is how continuity preserves itself.

But a culture shift toward proof does not stop there.

It matures.

People begin asking sharper questions.

If I want proof, why am I holding a claim.

If I want autonomy, why am I relying on a custodian.

If I want a hedge against the system, why is my hedge inside the system.

As those questions spread, the public starts distinguishing between exposure and ownership.

Between convenience and control.

That is when a cultural shift becomes a structural shift.

And that is what the silver canary is really warning about.

Not just inflation.

Not just debt.

Not just market stress.

A change in the public's relationship with money.

A change where proof becomes a mainstream value.

A change where abstraction becomes less acceptable.

A change where confidence management tools lose power because people stop buying the story without receipts.

When that happens, the system's options narrow.

It can offer more transparency.

It can offer stronger collateral.

It can rebuild credibility.

Or it can tighten control.

Those choices define the future.

Next, we step into what happens when the system's attempt to absorb the cultural shift collides with physical constraint.

Because you can package proof.

You can tokenize proof.

You can market proof.

You cannot create proof out of thin air.

And when a culture wants proof while supply is constrained, the transition is not smooth.

It is a repricing.

Not just of silver.

A repricing of trust itself.

Trust is the invisible asset that gets repriced first and noticed last.

CHAPTER 21

THE REPRICING OF TRUST

There are moments in history when the world still looks familiar, but the rules underneath it have already changed.

People still go to work.

Still buy groceries.

Still argue about politics.

Still laugh at memes.

Still make plans as if next month is guaranteed.

Then you notice the shift you cannot screenshot.

Trust has moved.

And when trust moves, everything reprices.

Not just assets.

Not just markets.

Life.

Because trust is the invisible asset underneath every visible asset.

Trust is why you accept a paycheck in dollars.

Trust is why you believe your savings will still matter when you need them.

Trust is why bonds can trade like safety instead of like risk.

Trust is why banks can operate on thin reserves without being challenged.

Trust is why digital balances feel like property instead of like access.

Trust is why paper promises can circulate as if they were substance.

Trust is the quiet agreement that makes modern finance possible at scale.

So when trust begins repricing, you do not just get a market cycle.

You get an era shift.

This is the moment we have been walking toward through every chapter.

The point where the silver story stops reading like a commodity story and starts reading like what it really is.

A trust story.

Because silver, at its core, is not about yield.

It is about belief.

Belief that currency can dilute.

Belief that policy can stretch beyond its stated limits.

Belief that systems can fracture under pressure.

Belief that physical reality matters more than narrative when stress rises.

Belief that proof has value when promises get loud.

When those beliefs spread, trust begins to migrate.

And migration is the repricing.

Repricing is what happens when an old assumption becomes too expensive to maintain.

It is what happens when risk that used to be hidden becomes impossible to ignore.

It is what happens when safe enough stops feeling safe.

It is what happens when paper no longer feels like a reliable proxy for reality.

Here is the crucial point.

Trust does not disappear all at once.

It relocates.

It shifts in layers.

It moves from one institution to another.

From one asset class to another.

From one narrative to another.

From convenience to certainty.

That movement is what creates volatility.

Think of trust like water and the world like containers.

In stable eras, trust sits comfortably in the largest containers.

Currency.

Banks.

Government debt.

Major institutions.

The public barely thinks about it.

The waterline feels permanent.

In unstable eras, trust starts leaking.

At first slowly.

Then faster.

It leaks into hard assets.

It leaks into redundancy.

It leaks into tangible stores of value.

It leaks into alternative rails.

It leaks into anything that feels less dependent on permission and promises.

The leak is the repricing.

Because when trust drains from one container, the value of that container changes.

Not instantly.

Inevitably.

Silver becomes unusually sensitive during this kind of migration because it sits at the intersection of three trust shifts happening at once.

Trust in currency stability.

Trust in market integrity.

Trust in supply adequacy.

When trust in currency thins, silver gets bid.

When trust in paper integrity thins, physical silver gets bid.

When trust in supply adequacy thins, availability becomes the headline.

That is why silver moves can feel disproportionate when they arrive.

It is rarely one story pushing the metal.

It is convergence.

And convergence creates force.

It is also why silver can exhaust people for long stretches.

Trust migrations are not straight lines.

They come in bursts.

They arrive in waves.

Denial.

Recognition.

Urgency.

Temporary calm.

Then another wave.

You can almost map the cycle by how the public learns.

A few hedge quietly.

Inflation becomes undeniable.

Behavior adjusts.

Proof gets sought.

The system answers with reassurance and intervention.

The reassurance stops matching lived reality.

Demand shifts again, stronger.

Control mechanisms tighten.

Physical assets gain status.

Strategic buyers secure supply.

Constraints show up.

Paper strains.

The gap between paper and physical becomes visible.

Then repricing.

And once repricing happens, the public learns something it does not unlearn.

The baseline changes.

In the old world, holding most of your value in currency felt normal.

In the new world, it feels fragile.

In the old world, trusting institutions felt normal.

In the new world, it feels conditional.

In the old world, paper exposure felt close enough to ownership.

In the new world, it reads like counterparty risk.

In the old world, the system will always work felt safe.

In the new world, it will probably work becomes the best most people can honestly say.

That psychological baseline is the repricing of trust.

And once it shifts, it touches everything.

Real estate.

Equities.

Bonds.

Commodities.

Currencies.

Crypto.

Precious metals.

Because every asset is, in some way, a reflection of where trust is being stored.

Now we need to be blunt about why this is destabilizing.

A paper system has flexibility as long as trust is thick.

When trust is thick, the system can absorb mistakes.

It can absorb debt.

It can absorb inflation.

It can absorb bailouts.

It can absorb political chaos.

Because the public still believes in the structure.

When trust thins, every mistake gets more expensive.

Every intervention gets more visible.

Every policy move gets more sensitive.

The system loses margin.

It loses room.

And when the system loses room, it reaches for control to replace what trust used to provide.

That is the loop.

Trust weakens.

Control increases.

Resistance grows.

Proof becomes cultural.

Trust migrates further.

The cycle tightens.

This is why trust repricing is not one dramatic event.

It is a new dynamic.

The world moving from a high-trust monetary regime into a managed-trust regime.

A regime where stability becomes more engineered.

A regime where proof becomes more valuable.

A regime where silver plays a larger role than most people expect.

Now land this with clarity, not fear.

If you feel like the world is unstable, your senses are not broken.

The system is evolving.

The social contract around money is being renegotiated.

Renegotiations always feel like confusion before they feel like direction.

And here is the opportunity hidden inside that discomfort.

When trust reprices, it redraws the map.

You see what is real.

You see what is dependent.

You see what is durable.

You see what needs hedging.

You see what you can control.

Silver fits into that clarity for a simple reason.

It is one of the cleanest forms of proof in a world where proof is becoming premium.

So the repricing of trust is the point where the silver canary's song stops sounding like a niche warning and starts sounding like the soundtrack of the era.

Real value.

Real ownership.

Real collateral.

Real weight.

Next, we take everything we have built and answer the question every reader is carrying, even if they have not said it out loud.

So what do I do.

Not as a trade.

As a strategy.

As a person.

As a family.

As someone building a future in a world that is learning, again, what trust costs.

You do not need certainty.

You need structure and options.

CHAPTER 22

SO WHAT DO YOU DO?

If you have made it this far, you are not reading for entertainment anymore.

You are reading because something in you already knows the world is shifting.

Maybe you do not have the perfect words for it yet.

Maybe you do not have the full map.

But you have felt it.

In the cost of living.

In the way institutions speak.

In the way policies snap into place.

In the way people behave when pressure rises.

In the way the future feels less like a straight line and more like a weather system.

And every reader eventually hits the same question.

So what do I do.

Not as a trader.

As a human with a life.

A family.

A business.

A future.

A nervous system that can only carry so much uncertainty before it starts demanding a plan.

This is where we make everything practical.

Not with a magic formula.

Not with bravado.

With something far more useful in a transition era.

A way to think clearly when clarity is rare.

Start here.

The goal is not to predict the future perfectly.

The goal is to reduce fragility.

The goal is to build options.

The goal is to create a posture that can survive multiple scenarios without requiring you to guess which headline wins next.

That is what intelligent positioning looks like.

If you have ever built anything in the real world, you already understand this.

You do not build a house for one perfect day of weather.

You build it for decades of weather.

Heat.

Cold.

Rain.

Wind.

Storms.

You plan for stress.

You reinforce.

You create redundancy.

You respect reality instead of betting your life on perfect conditions.

Financial resilience is the same kind of build.

It is structural.

It is boring in the way durable things are boring.

It is not a hot tip, a prediction, or a meme.

It is a posture.

Here is the posture, step by step.

1. Stop mistaking familiarity for safety

Familiarity is comfort.

Comfort is what keeps people on default settings.

Default settings work in stable eras.

In transition eras, default settings are where fragility hides.

If this book has taught you anything, it is that safe is not a label.

Safe is a relationship.

And in a trust repricing era, relationships change.

So the first move is mental.

You shift from passive trust to active awareness.

You stop assuming.

You start verifying.

You learn to see risk in layers instead of waiting for one dramatic event to announce itself.

2. Build liquidity you control

Liquidity is not just money.

It is access.

And access is what becomes conditional when systems get stressed.

This does not mean living in fear or turning your home into a bunker.

It means keeping enough flexibility in forms that do not break easily.

Immediate cash for short term needs.

Redundancy in where it is stored.

Multiple rails for moving value.

No single point of failure where one institution, one platform, one login, one policy change can lock your life.

That kind of redundancy feels boring until the day it feels like oxygen.

3. Reduce high interest debt like your future depends on it

Because it does.

Debt in stable eras is annoying.

Debt in volatile eras is a trap with teeth.

High interest debt compounds stress.

It eats margin.

It turns mild disruption into emergency.

People dislike this advice because it lacks dopamine.

Resilience does not care about dopamine.

Resilience cares about clean structure.

In the era we are entering, clean structure is a superpower.

4. Diversify stores of value by behavior, not by hype

Diversification is not own one of everything.

It is owning assets that respond differently under different stress conditions.

In a trust repricing era, you want a mix that covers multiple worlds.

Assets that hold up under inflation pressure.

Assets that hold up under deflationary shocks.

Assets that reduce counterparty risk.

Assets that remain liquid in normal life.

Assets that remain meaningful if rails tighten.

That last category is where most people are underprepared, because it forces an honest question.

If ownership becomes more like authorized access, what do you own that remains yours without requiring permission.

Now we can place silver correctly.

Silver is not the whole plan.

It is a tool inside the plan, and it is useful here for three reasons.

It gives you physical proof outside the rails.

It gives you exposure to the industrial backbone of the future.

It is accessible enough for normal people to build steadily.

But it must be held in the right frame.

Not as a get rich fantasy.

As a structural hedge.

If you treat it like a pillar, you buy it consistently.

You buy it patiently.

You expect frustration without letting frustration define your decisions.

You hold it for proof, not applause.

Insurance rarely feels exciting.

Insurance becomes priceless when it is needed.

5. Build redundancy in the rails you use

The future will not be one system.

It will be multiple systems running in parallel.

Traditional banking.

Digital payments.

New rails.

Tokenized assets.

Alternative settlement networks.

You do not need to become a tech wizard.

You do need to avoid single point dependence.

A resilient person has more than one way to store value.

More than one way to move value.

More than one way to access liquidity.

Redundancy does not create paranoia.

Redundancy creates options.

Options create calm.

6. Invest in skills that produce value in any macro environment

A lot of people prepare only by buying things.

Real resilience is also about what you can do.

Skills are portable value.

Skills travel across regimes.

Skills survive volatility.

Skills make you harder to control and harder to break.

Sales.

Negotiation.

Marketing.

Trades.

Systems thinking.

Tech literacy.

Emotional stability under pressure.

Leadership.

Communication.

Community building.

Part of your hedge should be you.

The stronger you are, the less dependent you are on any system remaining smooth.

7. Build community

This is the most underrated asset in any transition era.

People think preparation is individual.

It is not.

The strongest form of resilience is networked.

When supply chains strain, community matters.

When policies shift, community matters.

When systems tighten, community matters.

A person with assets but no relationships is fragile.

A person with relationships and skills is resilient even with fewer assets.

Now tie it together.

If you are asking what do I do, the answer is not one move.

The answer is structure.

Reduce fragility.

Build options.

Hold proof.

Diversify rails.

Grow skills.

Strengthen community.

Do it step by step, without drama, because resilience is not a reaction.

It is a build.

And here is the clean principle to carry forward.

In a world where trust is being repriced, your job is to own options that do not depend on trust remaining thick.

That is the strategy.

That is the posture.

That is why silver matters.

Next, we move into the final phase of the book by looking forward with realism, not fantasy.

What the next monetary era is likely to feel like.

What the new rails change.

What the silver war evolves into.

What happens when the world stops acting like the old system is permanent.

Because the future is not arriving someday.

It is already arriving.

And the canary has been singing the whole time.

The next era will not feel like a reset.

It will feel like a migration.

CHAPTER 23
THE NEXT MONETARY ERA

The future does not arrive like a parade.

It seeps in like water.

Quietly.

Through small decisions.

Through new technologies that feel like convenience.

Through policy changes that feel like updates.

Through cultural shifts that feel like "the way things are now."

Through the slow, almost boring realization that the old way of doing things is becoming too expensive to maintain.

Most people imagine a new monetary era begins with a declaration.

A summit.

A headline.

A moment where the world changes in public.

That is not how it works.

Monetary eras change the way continents drift.

You do not notice it day to day.

Then one day you look up and realize the map is different.

That is where we are.

The map is changing.

And if you have followed the logic of this book, you already know why.

Debt has grown past the point where it can be paid down the old way without tearing the system.

Interest costs have become a sensitivity, not a detail.

Inflation has become harder to kill without breaking something important.

Trust has thinned across institutions.

The world is fragmenting geopolitically.

Supply chains are becoming strategic.

New rails are being built.

The public is waking up to a truth it once ignored.

Money is not a neutral tool.

Money is power.

So when the map changes, what does it change into.

A clean replacement.

No.

The next era is a hybrid era.

A long overlap.

A messy coexistence.

A period where old money and new money run side by side.

Where legacy systems keep humming while new systems capture more territory.

Where people live in both worlds at once.

A multipolar monetary order.

A less singular reserve architecture.

A less uniform definition of money.

Not a switch.

An evolution.

To understand the next era, you have to understand the system's central dilemma.

The old system needs two things to function.

Expansion, because debt based systems stabilize through growth.

Trust, because paper promises require belief.

But expansion is running into limits.

And trust is being repriced.

So the system must evolve.

And systems evolve the same way organisms evolve under threat.

They reduce dependency on fragile inputs.

They build new mechanisms.

They tighten feedback loops.

They increase manageability.

That means digitization.

Tokenization.

Faster settlement.

More monitoring.

More enforceability.

More programmability.

This is not a conspiracy.

It is the predictable structural response of any machine trying to keep running while its tolerance for error shrinks.

If you were running a system that depended on fragile confidence, you would want tighter control too.

You would want faster intervention.

Better monitoring.

Fewer unknowns.

Fewer exits.

Most people would accept it, because it would be packaged as modernization and safety.

That brings us to the defining features of the next monetary era.

1. Money becomes increasingly digital and programmable

Not overnight.

Not through one dramatic rollout.

Through steady capture.

More transactions get tracked.

More payments route through centralized rails.

More settlement becomes software.

More policy becomes code.

This is bigger than convenience.

It is enforceability.

A programmable system gives institutions the ability to shape behavior precisely.

That is irresistible in volatile eras.

Digital rails become policy rails.

That is the shift.

2. Settlement becomes multipolar

The world is already moving away from a single unquestioned settlement architecture.

Not because the dollar disappears tomorrow.

Because nations want options.

Redundancy against sanctions.

Redundancy against policy unpredictability.

Redundancy against reserve risk.

So you see more bilateral trade outside old frameworks.

More alternative clearing networks.

More local currency settlement.

More reserve diversification.

More emphasis on commodities and collateral.

Multipolar does not mean instant collapse.

It means contested dominance.

And contested systems are volatile.

3. Hard collateral becomes more important

In high trust eras, paper can substitute for collateral because promises are believed.

In lower trust eras, collateral becomes premium because promises get questioned.

The next era values collateral more.

Not just among individuals.

Among institutions.

Among nations.

Among players who understand that when trust thins, the difference between a claim and a thing becomes decisive in the plumbing.

Gold remains the reserve collateral of history.

Silver becomes the collateral of modern industry.

Because this next era is not only monetary.

It is technological.

The world is building an electrified, digitized, hardware heavy future.

And the future runs on materials.

Silver's strategic value rises in two directions at once.

As proof when monetary trust thins.

As an input when industrial competition intensifies.

That dual role makes silver unusually potent in a hybrid era.

4. The public gets squeezed between inflation and control

This is the tradeoff the system is moving toward.

If the system keeps printing, inflation pressure persists.

If the system tightens aggressively, something breaks.

So the system tries to thread the needle.

Enough inflation management to maintain social stability.

Enough control to keep behavior predictable.

The result is a slow squeeze.

Not necessarily hyperinflation.

But enough erosion to make people feel it.

Not necessarily open authoritarianism.

But enough conditionality to make opting out harder.

That squeeze shapes culture.

It shapes behavior.

It shapes what people value.

Proof starts feeling like dignity.

5. The silver war intensifies

Not because silver becomes trendy.

Because silver becomes necessary.

Industrial demand rises.

Strategic procurement rises.

Public proof demand rises.

Supply stays constrained.

That combination is not stable.

It produces stress events.

Premium spikes.

Availability gaps.

Delivery friction.

Repricing moments.

And each repricing teaches the public.

Each visible gap between paper price and physical reality trains a new habit.

The war intensifies through feedback loops.

Now here is the most important insight about the next era.

It is not about choosing old or new.

It is about understanding that both will exist.

And the tension between them creates both risk and opportunity.

Old rails still matter.

New rails keep growing.

Hard assets reassert relevance.

Digital systems expand.

Trust is managed.

Proof is prized.

This hybrid world is messy.

But messiness is where repricing happens.

Messiness is where maps get redrawn.

Messiness is where people who understand structure can position themselves without needing to predict the exact day the weather shifts.

And this is where a new kind of literacy becomes essential.

In the old era, most people could ignore monetary mechanics and still do fine.

In the new era, ignoring monetary mechanics becomes expensive.

The next era rewards people who think in layers.

Who build redundancy.

Who diversify rails.

Who hold proof.

Who understand the difference between ownership and access.

Who understand that stability will be engineered, not guaranteed.

That is the central truth.

The next era will feel like a constant negotiation.

Between freedom and control.

Between scarcity and abstraction.

Between proof and convenience.

Between multipolar power and legacy dominance.

Silver sits inside that negotiation as both signal and tool.

So silver will not simply go up.

Silver will become part of the story the world tells itself about what money is.

And when an asset becomes part of that story, it does not just move.

It matters.

Next, we bring this book into its final movement.

Because now we have to answer the deepest question.

What is the endgame.

Not in a sensational way.

In a structural way.

What does the system want.

What does the public want.

What happens when those collide.

What role does silver play when the world decides what it values next.

That is where we end this journey.

The endgame is simple.

Whoever controls settlement controls the future.

CHAPTER 24

THE ENDGAME

If you want to understand where this goes, stop watching headlines and start watching incentives.

Headlines are weather.

Incentives are climate.

Headlines change by the hour. Incentives stay welded to the structure. Incentives tell you what institutions do when pressure rises. Incentives tell you what governments do when stability feels threatened. Incentives tell you what banks do when confidence weakens. Incentives tell you what people do when their lives feel less secure.

That is the endgame.

Not a single cinematic event.

A sequence of predictable moves.

A system trying to survive. A public trying to stay free enough to live.

Two endgames are unfolding at the same time.

The system's endgame.

And the people's endgame.

The next era is the collision between them.

The system's endgame: continuity

Start with the system.

The system's endgame is not evil. It is simple.

Continuity.

A modern debt based economy cannot tolerate mass instability. It cannot tolerate unpredictable behavior at scale. It cannot tolerate large portions of the public exiting the rails. It cannot tolerate a currency confidence spiral. It cannot tolerate a sudden repricing of collateral that exposes how levered the structure really is.

Because the moment the public truly sees how thin the margin of error is, the public starts making micro-decisions that turn theoretical risk into real crisis.

So the system's endgame becomes continuity through manageability.

That means three things.

First, digital rails that reduce friction and increase visibility.

Because visibility becomes control, and control becomes stability when trust thins.

Second, policy tools that can respond faster than markets can panic.

Because speed beats fear until fear learns to move faster than speed.

Third, incentive structures that keep the public participating.

Because participation is the oxygen of the fiat structure.

That is the system's direction.

A world where money is easier to manage, easier to trace, easier to stimulate, easier to restrict, easier to standardize, and harder to withdraw from.

Not because the system wants to punish everyone.

Because the system wants to prevent collapse.

But here is the catch.

Systems that prioritize continuity above all else drift toward control.

And control always charges a fee.

The fee is autonomy.

The people's endgame: dignity

That brings us to the people.

The people's endgame is not evil either. It is simple.

Dignity.

People want their work to mean something.

They want their savings to hold value.

They want to plan a future that does not get rewritten by policy.

They want to move freely.

They want to protect their families.

They want options.

They want ownership that behaves like property, not like authorized access.

That is the people's endgame.

And in a world where money becomes more programmable, the people's endgame becomes more urgent.

Because dignity requires optionality.

If you cannot opt out, you are not truly free.

You are comfortable.

And comfort can be revoked.

So the endgame is a tug of war between continuity and dignity.

Continuity says: stay inside the system and we will keep it stable.

Dignity says: I need options outside the system, even if I hope I never use them.

That tug of war is exactly where silver lives.

Silver is not only a hedge against inflation.

Silver is a hedge against the endgame itself.

Because the endgame is not only monetary.

It is behavioral.

It is about whether you live in a world where ownership is real, or a world where ownership is permission with a nicer user interface.

The compromise becomes the battlefield

Now for the part most people avoid, because it is uncomfortable.

The system cannot allow full autonomy in a fragile trust era without risking instability.

And the people cannot tolerate full control without losing dignity.

So the compromise becomes the battlefield.

It looks like this.

The system offers convenience so good it feels like mercy.

Instant payments.

Seamless settlement.

Frictionless life.

Rewards for participation.

Integrated finance.

Benefits that make opting out feel like self-sabotage.

And in exchange, the system expects compliance.

Not loud compliance.

Soft compliance.

The kind you do without noticing, because it feels normal, modern, safe.

This is how the endgame becomes a lifestyle.

You do not see it as a cage.

You see it as a platform.

Until you try to leave.

That is when the bars become visible.

That is why physical proof matters in the endgame.

Proof gives you leverage.

Not political leverage.

Personal leverage.

Proof gives you breathing room.

Proof gives you optionality.

Proof gives you an exit that does not require you to detonate your own life.

The endgame is a managed transition

Most people assume the endgame is a single new currency, a reset, a replacement, a dramatic moment.

More likely, it is a managed transition.

A hybrid era where old systems remain while new systems steadily dominate.

The system does not want chaos.

It wants controlled evolution.

Normalize programmability.

Reduce cash usage.

Increase digital dependence.

Make opt-outs inconvenient.

Do it slowly enough that people accept it as progress.

Progress is the easiest story to sell.

So the endgame is not a switch being flipped.

It is a direction.

A steady tightening of rails.

A steady cultural shift toward proof at the same time.

That is why this era is volatile.

Control increases.

Demand for proof increases.

Those forces collide in markets, in policy, in culture, and in living rooms.

And they collide inside silver because silver is both an opt-out and an input.

Silver becomes a referendum

Here is the crucial detail.

In the endgame, silver becomes more than a metal.

It becomes a referendum.

Not a political referendum.

A reality referendum.

A referendum on whether scarcity still matters.

A referendum on whether paper can substitute for substance indefinitely.

A referendum on whether the system's claims remain credible.

Because when silver gets tight, it reveals the limit of abstraction.

And the endgame is built on keeping abstraction smooth.

Smooth abstraction keeps participation high.

Silver is rough abstraction.

It is physical. Finite. Unmoved by narrative. Unmoved by policy. Unmoved by programming.

It forces the system to look at constraint.

And constraint is the enemy of a managed story.

Constraints force repricing.

Repricing forces awareness.

Awareness changes behavior.

Behavior forces tighter management.

That is the feedback loop.

Here is a line that separates early era from late era.

There is a difference between a system that is stable and a system that is being stabilized.

In the early era, stability felt native.

In the late era, stability has to be produced.

And in a produced stability regime, the public becomes a variable to manage, because the public can destabilize the structure through behavior.

That is why programmability matters.

That is why surveillance matters.

That is why incentives matter.

That is why friction shows up exactly where people try to exit.

That is why physical proof becomes the quiet form of resistance.

Landing the chapter

The endgame is not about whether silver wins.

The endgame is about whether people retain meaningful optionality.

Optionality is dignity.

Optionality is autonomy.

Optionality is the ability to live without fearing that a system update rewrites your life.

Silver is not a perfect solution.

But it is one of the most accessible forms of optionality an ordinary person can hold.

Not because it will make you rich.

Because it can keep you free enough to stay sane.

The future will be shaped by two forces.

The rails power builds.

And the proof people choose.

If the rails are fair, transparent, and stable, trust can be rebuilt.

If the rails are restrictive, opaque, and manipulative, proof becomes cultural faster.

That is the fork.

Silver sits at the fork as a signal.

So the endgame is not a date on a calendar.

It is a direction.

Toward programmability.

Toward multipolar rails.

Toward strategic materials.

Toward proof.

Toward the repricing of trust.

And your question as the reader is not will this happen.

It is how do I live wisely inside it.

The people who thrive in transition eras are not the people who panic.

They build structure.

They reduce fragility.

They keep options alive.

They own proof.

That is what this book is really doing.

It is not selling fear.

It is handing you a map.

And when you can read the signal, you stop reacting and start positioning.

CHAPTER 25

THE LAYERS THAT DECIDE EVERYTHING

When I was younger, I thought money was math.

Numbers.

Balances.

A paycheck.

A budget.

Bills paid on time.

A scoreboard that told you whether you were winning or losing.

Back then, money felt external, like weather.

You did not control it.

You adapted.

More money meant more ease.

Less meant more pressure.

Simple.

Then I held my first gold coin.

It was not just weight.

It was truth.

Not the kind of truth you debate.

The kind you feel in your hand.

Dense.

Quiet.

Unimpressed by your opinions.

Unmoved by headlines.

Unchanged by politics.

That moment cracked something open that took years to fully name.

Money is not math first.

Money is trust first.

Math comes later.

Money is the agreement we all make, consciously or unconsciously, that this symbol, this paper, this digital number, this promise is real enough to trade our lives for.

Once you see money as trust, the world stops looking random.

Every major financial event becomes legible.

A crisis is trust collapsing.

A boom is trust expanding.

A bubble is trust inflated beyond reality.

A recession is trust recalibrating.

A bailout is trust being propped up.

A devaluation is trust leaking.

A new rail is trust being rerouted.

Once you see it, you stop being shocked by what the world does.

You begin expecting it.

Because systems behave predictably under stress.

So do people.

That is why this final chapter matters.

You did not read this book to memorize facts.

You read it to upgrade your map.

To see the chaos without being pulled into it.

To understand what is actually happening when the language gets smooth and the outcomes get rough.

So here is the framework that ties everything together.

The mental model you can carry into the next decade.

Not as fear.

As structure.

I call it the **Three Layer Reality of Money**.

Layer One. Narrative.

Layer Two. Rails.

Layer Three. Reality.

If you understand these layers, you can understand every cycle, every surprise, every pivot, every crackdown, every repricing.

You can understand why silver matters.

You can position yourself without panic.

Layer One: Narrative

Narrative is what you are told.

The official story.

The explanation for what is happening and why it is fine.

The language of temporary.

The language of contained.

The language of strong fundamentals.

The language of nothing to see here.

Narrative is not always a lie.

Narrative is selection.

It is the portion of truth that keeps behavior calm.

Because calm is valuable.

Calm keeps people working.

Calm keeps people saving.

Calm keeps people investing.

Calm keeps people paying taxes, mortgages, student loans, insurance premiums.

Calm keeps the machine upright.

That is why narrative is the first line of defense for any monetary system.

If the narrative holds, the system holds.

When people believe the story, behavior makes the story real.

This is why narrative manufacturing matters.

When narrative becomes programmable, perception becomes a policy tool.

Here is the key.

Narrative is the softest layer.

It is also the most influential layer for most people.

Most people live inside narrative.

They absorb it.

They repeat it.

They build their plans on it.

Until narrative and lived experience drift too far apart.

When the gap becomes personal, narrative breaks.

And when narrative breaks, people go looking for something harder.

That takes us to the next layer.

Layer Two: Rails

Rails are the systems that move value.

Banks.

Payment networks.

Settlement systems.

Trading platforms.

Custody structures.

Regulations.

The pipes.

The rules.

The mechanisms.

In stable eras, rails feel invisible.

You swipe your card.

Your paycheck lands.

Your rent clears.

You do not think about plumbing when the water is hot.

In transition eras, rails become visible.

Because rails become political.

Rails become strategic.

Rails become programmable.

Rails become enforceable.

Rails become the tools power uses when narrative alone cannot hold behavior in place.

This is when confidence becomes policy.

This is when intervention becomes normal.

This is when temporary turns into infrastructure.

This is when money starts behaving less like property and more like access.

Rails define what you can do.

How fast you can do it.

Where you can do it.

Whether you can do it at all.

Rails can increase freedom.

They can also increase manageability.

And in a trust thinning era, manageability becomes the priority.

That is why rails are being rebuilt.

That is why alternative settlement keeps growing.

That is why digital currency infrastructure keeps expanding.

That is why programmability shows up dressed as convenience.

Here is the key.

Rails can be upgraded.

Rails can be controlled.

Rails can be changed.

But rails cannot defeat the final layer.

Layer Three: Reality

Reality is what exists.

Not what you are told exists.

Not what an app says exists.

Not what a contract claims exists.

What exists.

Scarcity.

Physics.

Materials.

Energy.

Food.

Land.

Labor.

Silver.

Gold.

Reality is where promises have to cash out.

Reality is where paper meets limits.

Reality is where leverage meets constraint.

Reality is where abstraction must settle.

Reality is why you can print liquidity but cannot print trust.

Reality is why you can build new rails but cannot rail your way out of scarcity.

Reality is why the silver canary sings.

Because silver lives on the seam between rails and reality.

It is a monetary metal and an industrial necessity.

It is physical proof and modern utility.

It is scarcity with a job.

Silver is where the system's story can be tested.

Try to buy it.

Try to take delivery.

Watch premiums.

Watch availability.

Watch how the physical market behaves while the narrative stays calm.

That is reality speaking.

And reality always wins eventually.

It can be delayed.

It can be managed.

It can be softened with language.

It cannot be permanently denied.

So the framework is simple.

Narrative.

Rails.

Reality.

Now watch what happens in every era shift.

Narrative starts breaking.

Rails start changing.

Reality starts forcing repricing.

That is the story you have been reading the whole time.

The silver war is reality pushing back against narrative through physical constraint.

The programmable cage is rails evolving to maintain continuity when trust thins.

The rush toward proof is people moving toward reality when narrative weakens and rails feel controllable.

The repricing of trust is the moment reality forces the system to admit what narrative tried to smooth.

Once you see the layers, you stop reacting to noise.

You start watching signals.

And the signal is almost always the same.

When reality diverges from narrative, something is cracking.

Silver is one of the first places that divergence shows up.

Not because it predicts everything.

Because it reveals stress early.

The Anchors That Hold

Understanding is not enough.

You need anchors.

In a world where narrative is engineered, rails are programmable, and reality is constrained, what do you anchor your life to.

Five things.

Liquidity you control.

Reduced fragility.

Hard collateral.

Skills and value creation.

Community.

Those anchors are not theory.

They are what people build in every transition era, whether they call it preparation or common sense.

Combine the layers with the anchors, and you have a complete map.

You can hear what is being said.

You can see how the system is changing.

You can feel what is real enough to hold through uncertainty.

That is the point of this book.

Not to scare you.

To upgrade you.

So let me leave you with an image.

Imagine walking through a building you have lived in your whole life.

You know every hallway.

Every door.

Every sound.

You never think about exits.

Then one day the lights flicker.

Not a blackout.

Just enough to pause.

A fire alarm chirps once and stops.

A hallway smells faintly like smoke.

Nobody runs.

Most people keep walking.

Some laugh.

Some ignore it.

But you stop.

You do not panic.

You notice.

You glance toward the exits.

You make a quiet plan.

You keep moving, but differently.

That is what this book was meant to do.

Not to turn you into a doomer.

To turn you into a builder with awareness.

The silver canary is the flicker.

The premium spike.

The delivery delay.

The narrative mismatch.

The policy intervention.

The tightening rails.

The cultural shift toward proof.

Those signals do not mean the building is guaranteed to burn.

They mean the building is under stress.

And in stressed buildings, people with a plan do not panic.

They move intelligently.

That is you now.

You have the map.

You understand the layers.

You understand why silver matters.

You understand the direction.

And you understand the difference between a story and a structure.

So carry this forward.

Watch the narrative.

Watch the rails.

Watch reality.

And own enough proof that no matter what story gets told next, your life remains yours.

Most people cannot name it.

But they feel it.

The sensation that the rules are changing.

They are.

EPILOGUE

THE WEIGHT OF WHAT'S REAL

There is a moment I still remember with odd clarity.

Nothing dramatic happened. No crash. No sirens. No headlines screaming in the background. Just a quiet day that became unforgettable because of something small.

A coin.

I had held "money" my whole life. Paper bills. Plastic cards. Digital balances. It all felt normal, like breathing. I never questioned it because I never had to. It worked. You earn it, you save it, you spend it, you repeat.

Then I held a real ounce of metal for the first time, and something in me shifted.

It was the weight.

Not in the poetic sense. In the literal sense. The dense, undeniable reality that does not care who is in office, what the chart looks like, or what the talking heads are selling today. The silent presence of something that exists without permission.

That coin did not promise me anything.

It did not offer interest.

It did not flash graphs.

It did not pitch itself as a "solution."

It simply sat in my hand and told the truth without words.

This is real.

And I remember thinking, almost embarrassed by how obvious it felt.

So much of the world is built on things you cannot hold.

Contracts.

Policies.

Confidence.

Reputation.

Credit.

Forecasts.

Models.

Numbers on screens.

Most of the time, that is fine. That is how modern life functions. But there are seasons when you start noticing how much of your stability depends on everyone agreeing that the invisible is solid.

In those seasons, the human mind starts searching for anchors.

That is what this book has been about.

Not fear.

Anchors.

Because whether people admit it or not, a quiet anxiety is spreading through modern life. It is not always loud enough to call panic, but it is there. You can hear it in how people talk about the cost of living. You can feel it in how quickly conversations get tense when politics comes up. You can see it in the distrust toward the news, institutions, and even each other. You can sense it in the way the future feels less predictable than it used to.

Most people cannot name it, but they feel it.

It is the sensation that the rules are changing.

And the truth is, they are.

Not because someone flipped a villain switch.

Because systems evolve when they get stretched.

Debt stretches systems.

Inflation stretches systems.

Geopolitics stretches systems.

Technology stretches systems.

Trust, once stretched far enough, starts to thin.

And when trust thins, the whole world becomes more sensitive. More reactive. More fragile.

That is why silver matters.

Not because it is a magic metal.

Because it lives at the intersection of what the system says and what the system can deliver.

Silver has a peculiar gift.

It tells the truth about stress early.

It reveals when supply is tighter than the narrative implies.

It reveals when people begin valuing proof more than promises.

It reveals when confidence starts leaking out of the abstraction layer and moving toward things that can be held.

It is a canary.

Not because it predicts the exact day of a collapse.

Because it sings when the air is changing.

And the air is changing.

You do not need to be an economist to see it.

You can see it in your grocery cart.

You can see it in your mortgage rate.

You can see it in your insurance bill.

You can see it in the way the world feels like it is moving faster, tightening faster, reacting faster.

You can see it in the way "normal" has started requiring more explanation.

That is what late era systems feel like.

They still function, but they require more management. More intervention. More narrative. More policy. More control.

And the public can sense the difference between a system that is stable and a system that is being stabilized.

That difference creates the quiet shift.

The shift toward proof.

The shift toward options.

The shift toward personal redundancy.

Not because people want to fight the world.

Because people want to survive the world.

And survival is not always dramatic.

Sometimes survival is owning enough reality that you can breathe calmly when the screens start shouting.

That is what I hope this book gave you.

A calmer nervous system.

A clearer map.

A framework you can use to interpret what is happening without getting dragged by every headline.

Because you are going to see more noise.

More campaigns.

More certainty packaged in flashy language.

More "experts" who speak like the future is settled.

And the temptation will always be the same.

React.

Chase.

Panic.

But the people who thrive in transition eras are not the people who react fastest.

They are the people who think deepest.

They are the people who keep their structure clean.

They are the people who build a life with options.

They are the people who own enough proof that they do not need permission to remain stable.

So let me leave you with something simple, because it is simple.

As the world shifts, you do not need to guess perfectly.

You need to position intelligently.

Reduce fragility.

Build redundancy.

Hold assets you control.

Develop skills that create value.

Invest in relationships that make life stronger.

And yes, own some form of proof.

Silver is one of the most accessible forms of proof the average person can hold.

It is not a religion.

It is not a conspiracy.

It is a strategy.

A form of personal collateral in a world where collateral is becoming important again.

Because here is the truth nobody can escape.

Even in a digital future, the physical world still runs on physical things.

You can build new rails.

You can build new currencies.

You can build new systems.

You cannot code your way out of scarcity.

You cannot digitize your way out of materials.

You cannot program your way out of reality.

Reality remains the final layer.

Reality is what every promise eventually has to meet.

That is why proof will matter more.

That is why the canary will keep singing.

That is why the next era will reward people who understand the difference between narrative, rails, and reality.

And that is why I wrote this.

I do not want you walking into the next decade sleepwalking.

I do not want you trapped inside someone else's story.

I do not want you relying on default settings designed for an era that is fading.

I want you awake.

Calm.

Clear.

Prepared.

Not with fear.

With structure.

I want you to feel the weight of what is real.

Because once you do, you stop being easily manipulated by what is not.

So as you close this book, let the world keep doing what it does.

Let headlines rise and fall.

Let narratives shift.

Let rails evolve.

Let noise continue.

You do not need to fight it.

You just need to see it.

And if you can see it, you can position yourself.

You can protect your family.

You can preserve your autonomy.

You can build your future with your eyes open.

That is the whole point.

In the end, the silver canary is not telling you to panic.

It is telling you to pay attention.

Because attention is the first step to freedom.

And freedom is not a political slogan.

Freedom is having options.

Freedom is having proof.

Freedom is knowing that no matter how the system evolves, your life remains yours.

That is the weight of what is real.

And once you feel it, you never forget it.

Author's Note

Why I Wrote This

I did not set out to become the guy who talks about money at the party.

I did not wake up one morning and decide I wanted to spend my life thinking about currency collapse, precious metals, and the invisible mechanics that run the modern world.

I was a working man. I came from construction. I lived in the real world, where if you do not build it right, it breaks. If you do not measure twice, you pay for it. If you cut corners, the job eventually exposes you.

That kind of work wires your brain differently.

It teaches you to respect reality.

It teaches you that structure matters more than opinions.

It teaches you that weight, tension, and physics always win.

For a long time, money felt like the opposite of that world.

Money felt like symbols. Numbers. Forms. Paper. Screens. A game everyone played without asking too many questions.

I played it too.

Like most people, I assumed the system was stable because it had always been there.

Then I moved into sales.

At first it was car sales, which taught me something early.

Perception drives behavior.

People do not buy what is "true." They buy what they believe. They buy emotion, then justify it later. They buy stories.

That lesson mattered more than I realized at the time, because it was my first glimpse into how the world really works.

Later, I heard about precious metals sales for the first time. Someone mentioned how much money was being made selling gold and silver. At the time, I barely knew what that meant. I had heard the phrase "precious metals," but I filed it under history.

Then curiosity did what curiosity always does.

It pulled a thread.

I started investigating.

I learned what gold and silver actually were. Not as collectibles. As money. As anchors. As the original form of value that survived empires, resets, political cycles, and currency experiments.

And that investigation led me to the question that changes everything once you ask it honestly.

What is money.

That question is a rabbit hole.

It starts with economics and ends with power.

It starts with currency and ends with trust.

It starts with personal finance and ends with civilization.

Because once you understand fiat currency is backed by belief, not substance, you start noticing how fragile belief can be.

And once you notice fragility, you start watching the world differently.

You stop seeing politics as politics. You see monetary theater.

You stop seeing wars as wars. You see resource conflict and settlement power.

You stop seeing markets as neutral. You see incentives, mechanisms, and narrative.

You stop seeing inflation as a statistic.

You see it as the invisible tax that reshapes society.

I read everything I could. I studied. I sold. I listened. I learned.

I built a precious metals career. I opened a national brokerage. I watched patterns. I watched cycles. I watched how often the official story did not match the lived story. I watched how people react when the system gets stressed. I watched how quickly confidence can evaporate.

And I watched how consistently the same response appears whenever trust begins thinning.

People look for proof.

They look for something real.

They look for something that does not require permission to exist.

That is silver.

That is gold.

That is hard collateral.

That is why I wrote *The Silver Bomb*, and why this updated work exists.

Because the world is shifting again.

And this time the shift is not only about inflation.

It is about the evolution of money itself.

New rails. More programmability. A future where access can become conditional. A world where the line between ownership and permission becomes more important.

In that world, the value of proof rises.

This book is not an attempt to scare you.

It is an attempt to respect you.

To speak plainly.

To give you a framework.

To help you understand what you are seeing so you can make better decisions without panic.

If you are reading this, I assume you can sense the difference between comfort and stability.

You want a strategy, not a fantasy.

You want clarity, not hype.

You want to protect what you have built.

So here is my promise.

I wrote this as a working man, not a theorist.

I wrote it as someone who believes reality matters more than opinion.

I wrote it to be read cover to cover.

Not as a pile of facts.

As a story that upgrades your understanding of the world.

You do not need to agree with every conclusion to benefit from the framework.

If you finish this book with a clearer map and stronger structure, it did its job.

If you finish it feeling calmer, more prepared, and more capable of navigating the next decade, then it was worth writing.

Because the future belongs to the people who build resilience.

Quietly.

Intelligently.

One good decision at a time.

Thank you for reading.

And more importantly, thank you for being the kind of person who refuses to sleepwalk through a changing world.

THE SILVER CANARY CHECKLIST

A PRACTICAL TOOLKIT FOR READING THE SIGNAL

If you have made it this far, you have something most people never develop, even after a lifetime of watching markets.

You can see structure.

This section turns that structure into practical awareness. Think of it as a field guide you can reopen whenever the world gets loud, confusing, or unstable.

Use the Quickstart when you want speed. Use the full checklist when you want depth.

THE SILVER CANARY QUICKSTART

3 Signals. 3 Actions. 3 Mistakes.

You do not need to memorize the whole book.

You only need to recognize the early tells, act with calm precision, and avoid the traps that keep people stuck in reaction mode.

This is the fast version.

THE 3 SIGNALS

What shows up first

1 Premiums

When the screen price stays calm but physical costs more, stress is forming. The quote is losing authority.

2 Inventory

One dealer being out is normal. Multiple dealers being out at once is a market level signal. Scarcity is building.

3 Delivery

When "ships tomorrow" becomes "ships next week," and delays become routine, rationing has started quietly. Delays are the first form of shortage.

THE 3 ACTIONS

What to do with the signal

1 Stay grounded and verify reality

Do not debate the screen. Check premiums, availability, and delivery across multiple sources. Reality speaks first.

2 Reduce fragility

If your plan depends on perfect liquidity, perfect timing, or perfect stability, it is fragile. Strength comes from optionality.

3 Position before the crowd

The best time to build protection is before panic makes everything expensive. Move with structure, not urgency.

THE 3 MISTAKES

How people get trapped

1 Waiting for official confirmation

By the time the system admits stress, pricing has shifted and options have narrowed.

2 Confusing paper pricing for physical reality

The screen is a reference point. The physical market is the truth test.

3 Overreacting instead of building a framework

Stress makes people swing between denial and panic. A framework keeps you steady.

If you remember one thing, remember this:

When premiums rise, inventory thins, and delivery stretches, the canary is already singing.

And if you can hear it early, you can move early.

WHAT TO WATCH WHEN THE SYSTEM IS UNDER STRESS

Most people wait for permission to believe what they are already feeling.

They wait for a headline.

They wait for an official statement.

They wait for the screen price to confirm their instincts.

But stress shows up long before the story changes.

It shows up in gaps. In delays. In friction that suddenly becomes normal. In the way behavior changes while the language stays calm.

Over the years, I have learned the signal is rarely loud at first.

It is subtle.

It is the moment you try to do something simple, like place an order, and the world answers with an unexpected pause.

That pause matters.

This checklist teaches you how to read those pauses in real time.

A) SILVER SIGNALS

The canary

1 Premiums rise while spot stays calm

If the screen looks quiet but physical silver costs noticeably more, paper is losing control of the reference price. This is one of the earliest tells.

2 Inventory thins across multiple dealers at once

One dealer being out happens. Several dealers showing out of stock on similar products in the same window is a market signal, not a store issue.

3 Delivery times stretch and "backorder" becomes routine

Scarcity often arrives as delay before it arrives as price. If "two weeks" becomes "four to six," and "four to six" becomes "we will let you know," stress has moved from rumor to logistics.

4 Product substitution becomes normal

You order a specific bar or coin. They offer something "equivalent." That is supply pressure wearing a friendly mask.

5 The spread between buying and selling widens

A widening bid ask spread usually means dealers are protecting inventory and pricing uncertainty. It is the market charging you for risk.

6 Large orders get treated differently than small ones

If bigger orders require negotiation, sourcing, special approvals, or waitlists, the market has shifted from casual flow to constrained allocation.

B) MONEY + CREDIT SIGNALS

The pressure underneath everything

Silver is the canary, but credit is the oxygen. When credit tightens, everything behaves differently.

1 Rates stop acting like policy tools and start acting like alarms

In stable periods, rates feel guided. In stressed periods, rates feel like the market is grabbing the wheel.

2 Liquidity disappears where it used to be deep

Small headlines create outsized moves. Healthy systems absorb shocks. Fragile systems amplify them.

3 Credit tightens while optimism is advertised

Watch what lenders do. If standards tighten, approvals come with new conditions, or borrowing gets harder, caution is already in the pipes.

4 Rolling debt becomes harder

When refinancing costs rise, it is like raising the rent on the entire system. The problem is rarely the debt itself. The problem is the cost of carrying it.

5 Emergency measures become normal

When interventions shift from rare to routine, you are watching a system that needs constant maintenance to hold its shape.

C) NARRATIVE SIGNALS

When words start changing

You can learn a lot from tone. Not the content. The tone.

1 Messaging becomes coordinated

When every major voice starts using the same phrases, confidence is being managed. This does not automatically mean deception. It means stabilization is the priority.

2 New vocabulary appears

Transitory. Soft landing. Strong and resilient. When language shifts, it is often because the old language stopped working.

3 Reassurance replaces transparency

When officials promise outcomes instead of describing conditions, the truth is usually more complex than the sound bite.

4 The story focuses on isolated blame instead of systemic causes

Scapegoats appear when systems need cover. If the explanation feels too clean, reality is usually messier.

D) RAIL SHIFT SIGNALS

When the new system takes territory

This is where the book expands beyond silver, because money is not only currency.

Money is settlement.

Money is access.

Money is custody.

Money is control.

1 Settlement becomes strategic

When nations and institutions prioritize alternative rails, they are reducing dependence on the old system. That is positioning.

2 Custody becomes the headline

When who holds it becomes as important as what it is, ownership and permission are separating.

3 Digital identity expands quietly

The new system often arrives through convenience first. What begins as frictionless access can become conditioned access.

4 Programmable policy moves from theory to implementation

Once money can be programmed, behavior can be shaped. That does not guarantee dystopia. It guarantees a stronger incentive architecture.

5 Transparency rises while autonomy shrinks

This trade arrives disguised as security and efficiency. Once normalized, it becomes the baseline.

E) THE MOST IMPORTANT SIGNAL OF ALL

When the gap between what the screen says and what real life costs begins widening, you are watching the system reveal stress.

That gap is where the canary sings.

And if you learn to hear it, you stop needing permission to see what is coming.

You will already be positioned.

ABOUT THE AUTHOR

Michael MacDonald is a best-selling author, investor, and entrepreneur working at the intersection of money, trust, and emerging systems of value.

For decades, he has studied the fault lines of paper finance and the structural weaknesses of debt-based monetary systems, long before these risks entered mainstream conversation. His career began in the precious metals industry, where he helped individuals and families understand gold, silver, currency cycles, and the deeper question most people only ask when it matters:

What is money?

In 2012, Michael became an early participant in Bitcoin and the broader crypto ecosystem. He later expanded into Ethereum, tokenized systems, and the infrastructure now known as the Internet of Value. He was also an early pioneer in NFTs, exploring digital property rights and programmable ownership well before they entered public awareness.

Today, Michael is the creator of Sonic Supplements™ and the founder of HitZero.com, a platform at the intersection of AI, music, wellness, and blockchain. HitZero turns human intention into personalized sound designed to sharpen clarity, unlock flow, and elevate performance, while advancing a future where creativity, ownership, and monetization run on transparent, auditable rails.

Michael writes with one purpose: to bring clarity to a changing world, reveal the signal before the headlines, and help people understand the systems being built beneath the future of global value.

Learn more at TheSilverCanary.com
Listen at SilverCanaryRadio.com

www.ingramcontent.com/pod-product-compliance
Lightning Source LLC
LaVergne TN
LVHW052318200926
848481LV00002B/597